£4-95

THE
CHRISTMAS
CRAFTS BOOK

First published in Great Britain in 1979

© 1979 Search Press Limited, London
New edition, slightly abridged and reset 1981
Reprinted 1982
Reprinted in larger format 1984

The photographs and drawings in *The Christmas Crafts Book*
first appeared in different volumes of the Leisurecrafts and
Home-made series published by Search Press Limited,
Wellwood, North Farm Road, Tunbridge Wells,
Kent TN2 3DR;
and of the Brunnen-Reihe series published by
Christophorus-Verlag GmbH,
Freiburg im Breisgau, Federal Republic of Germany.
See detailed acknowledgements on page 126.

ISBN(C) 0 85532 545 3

ISBN(Pb) 0 85532 546 1

Made and printed in Spain by Editorial Elexpuru Hnos.,
Zamudio-Bilbao.

THE
CHRISTMAS
CRAFTS BOOK

SEARCH PRESS

CHRISTMAS CRAFTS

Contents

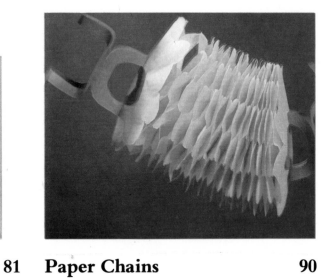

Introduction

Christmas, the most exciting celebration time of the year, is planned, thought about and looked forward to for weeks and even months in advance.

The time to start sending cards, thinking about gifts and planning decorations is the beginning of December. It is sensible for every craftsperson to gather together tools and materials and to start making nearly everything that goes with the celebration of the Nativity, well before Christmas Day.

Send your Christmas cards out in good time this year; you can even start making them in the summer. Collect and press flowers, and when they are dry, mount them up to make beautiful and unusual designs to go on the front cards. You can make prints, collages, drawings, anything you like to produce really special cards with a personal touch.

While collecting flowers, it is wise to look for plants and seeds, such as thistles and pine-cones, which you can dry and use for table centerpieces and room decorations. When arranged carefully with evergreen foliage, berries and candles, these attractive materials make original and distinctive displays, as good as any manufactured paper chain or balloon.

If you wish to be really original, try making your own paper chains. All you need is tissue paper, a template, a sharp knife and some glue. Once you have made a few, you can design your own to suit any room.

Candles add a warm and friendly glow to the Christmas season, whether you use them in a table centerpiece or for illumination. It is easy to make your own candles or candlesticks from the basic materials and use your own ideas for shapes and colors. You can soon have homemade candles flickering brightly.

Every year, children of all ages retell the Christmas story in words, music and pictures. A special section of this book shows how to make a Nativity scene with Mary and Joseph, Jesus, the Wise Men, animals and worshippers. Make the figures and properties from paste and paper, cloth, clay, wire, wood, stones, bark, twigs, and anything you can find that will offer a suitable recreation of the Nativity.

Make stars and angels from straw and metal foil as extra decorations to go anywhere in the house. Make the Christmas tree even more majestic, colorful and exciting with your own home-made decorations.

When Christmas Day arrives, and it is time to unwrap gifts, your friends and relatives will be even more delighted if you make the presents yourself.

All the work you do will make it a never-to-be-forgotten Christmas, and give pleasure and enjoyment to everyone concerned. You will find immense joy in making your own contribution to the Christmas season.

Table & room decorations

In some countries it is the custom, even before Christmas Day itself, to decorate the dining table and other furniture with decorative arrangements that proclaim the coming of light and festivity. Table and room decorations made from dried plants, fruits and cones add gaiety to any festive or party occasion, and they are particularly useful when fresh flowers are in short supply, or out of season and expensive to buy.

You can gather the materials for your arrangements from the countryside, your own garden, or specialist shops. But remember, even if you do have to pay for some of your materials, you can use them again and again in different combinations.

There are many methods for preserving flowers from your own garden—the simplest way is to dry them by hanging. Pick flowers on a very dry day when the flower head is young and not fully open. Seed heads should be gathered when they are beginning to dry on the plant. Tie the flowers in bunches, taking care that the flowers do not crush one another, and hang them upside down in a dry, dark, airy place—an airing cupboard is ideal—for two to three weeks. This method also works well with grasses and cereals. If gathered in the spring they will remain green, while later in the year they will be the familiar golden color.

Tools and materials

The simplicity of this craft means that very few new tools and materials need to be bought, as most of them are already to be found in the home. You will need a hammer, pliers (preferably pointed), a pair of wire-cutters, pruning shears, a few nails of various lengths, and possibly a simple hand-drill.

Gardening shops or florists will be able to supply you with florist's wire and green plasticized florist's tape, together with neutral or natural-colored raffia for binding. There are many materials available for supporting your arrangement—the best is florist's foam, but you can also use flower arranger's putty or a non-hardening modeling clay.

In addition to man-made containers, you should also consider natural objects as the basis for your display: tree roots, fungoid growths from trees, bark, a slice of wood from a tree trunk, parts of coconut shells, large sea shells or even slabs of slate or granite. Just let your imagination go to work and you will find that almost any visually pleasing natural object can be used in a decorative display.

The arrangements shown here are intended as sources of inspiration rather than examples which should be slavishly imitated. You may find that some of the plants used are not obtainable in your area, but that should not deter you from seeking out equally attractive substitutes. It is important that you obtain a variety of forms and materials. Try to arrange them on three levels, so that each flower head or blossom appears above another, and the larger, darker flowers are on the lowest level.

Always remember that each decoration should have a focal point—a center from which the components emerge, or towards which they point. In most cases this will be the florist's foam or modeling clay in which the plants have been inserted, or the container itself.

Some of the instructions refer to the process of wiring-up. This is important preparatory work which has to be done carefully if your arrangement is to last. It is especially important for pine and other cones or similar natural growths which do not have strong supporting stalks. To wire a cone, wrap a strong but pliable 125mm (5in.) wire round the base of the cone. Twist the two ends of the wire around each other, tightly against the cone, then all the way down to form a stalk.

A rustic arrangement of ruscus, berries, bleached cones, thistles and poppies, a red candle and a ribbon.

Make your own wreath by wiring ruscus on a circle of strong wire. You can then add more decorations.

Wiring-up.

When using wires to hold candles in position, heat them before inserting them into the candles.

Decorating a straw wreath with greenery.

If you are using everlasting flowers, cut off the stem and push a florist's wire through the center of the flower. Turn a small hook over at the top and draw this into the flower. The wire 'stem' can be disguised, if required, by slipping it into any hollow stem. Beech nuts are more easily wired up if the wire is led through a bead or a small everlasting flower which will form the center of the cluster. Many materials and plants, including aloe rings, lotus, fungus and loofah—cause no difficulties at all when wiring-up.

Rustic centerpiece

The rustic-looking arrangement on page 8 was inspired by the wooden container, which is actually a plant-pot holder bought from a flower shop. The materials used are a large red candle, ruscus (an evergreen shrub), berries, bleached cones, thistles, poppies and red ribbon.

Put some florist's foam in the base of the container. The candle is secured in the florist's foam by three thick wires which are heated and then pushed into the base of the candle at one end, and pressed into the florist's foam at the other. Ruscus is arranged thickly around the candle and then the berries, cones, poppies and thistles are added. The red ribbon bow is the final touch.

A straw wreath, which you can make or buy, decorated simply with red candles, four bleached cones, berries and fruits, and tartan ribbon bows.

Straw wreath

The straw wreath, which is used unadorned in the arrangement above, could also form the basis for the wreaths on pages 12 and 13. There are many types of wreath which can be bought from a florist. The simplest is a plastic foam hoop, but this needs a lot of material to cover it completely. You may find it easier to ask your florist to make up a simple moss wreath, similar to that shown on page 12, which only requires the minimum of additional decoration.

Very few materials were used for the straw wreath—four red candles, four bleached cones, berries and fruits and four tartan ribbon bows. The candles were attached by means of three thick wires inserted in their bases and then pushed into the straw.

Bead rings, painted and unpainted cones, ribbons and four candles are all you need to turn this plain florist's wreath into an attractive table centerpiece.

Blue cone wreath

The blue wreath above has some painted cones to echo the colors of the candles and ribbons. These have been painted at the tips with a brush, but you can also use an aerosol paint in one of the many colors available, including gold and silver, for an all-over color. Some bead rings, which are made by stringing alternate blue and white beads, have been added. The colors of these rings can be varied to suit the color of any particular arrangement.

A decorated ruscus wreath.

Ruscus wreath

The wreath above was made from the evergreen ruscus, whose dense foliage is ideal for covering a plastic foam base. In this case, it was wired to a strong wire circle as shown in the diagram, before being placed on a raffia mat to protect the table surface.

Fir-cone centerpiece

The pine-cone arrangement (*page 15, top*) has a mound of non-hardening modeling clay on a circular board as its base, which has then been completely obscured by the wired pine-cones, berries and candles.

For a small table you might like to use one of the attractive pyramids (*page 15, below*) as a centerpiece. The pyramid on the left is set on a raffia mat with a plastic foam ball decorated with ruscus, statice, bleached cones, berries and fruit, gold-painted cones and cypress. To attach a candle firmly, cut away the top from a plastic foam ball to give a flat surface. Then insert a candle with three wires in the base. All the other material is added until the ball is completely covered. Use a toothpick to pierce a hole for each piece as you are ready to place it. The fir pyramid on the right is constructed in the same way, and can be built on a raffia mat or plate which will be concealed when the arrangement is complete.

The fir sprigs can be inserted more easily if the first needles are removed and the ends are sharpened. The gilded beads have been wired separately and gathered into clumps, and moss has been used to fill in the remaining gaps.

Miniature Christmas tree

The three-candle arrangement on page 17 has a plain pottery dish as its base. In addition to a small tree complete with roots, the arrangement is made up from holly sprigs, moss, various types of pine-cones, berries and apples.

The Christmas tree is planted in sufficient soil to support it. The soil is then covered with moss which is wired to hold it in position. The candles are wired first, and then inserted firmly into the moss, and the holly, wired cones, berries and fruits arranged around the edge of the dish.

Lone pine

The unusual pine-cone tree *(right)* is simple to make and could decorate the corner of a room or a hallway. The trunk is made from a length of dowel, or a cut-down broomstick which has been wrapped in green crêpe paper. It can be painted if preferred, or alternatively made from a length of bamboo. The trunk is supported in a plant pot three-quarters filled with earth which is concealed on top by large stones.

The top of the tree is a large plastic foam ball painted brown with watercolor paint. After the paint is dry, pine-cones are glued in rows, the cones in each row sitting in the gaps left by the cones in the previous row. Make sure each row is glued firmly in position before going on to the next. Fill in the gaps between cones with wired berries or small fruits, and tie a wide ribbon in a bow, leaving long trailing ends, for the final festive touch.

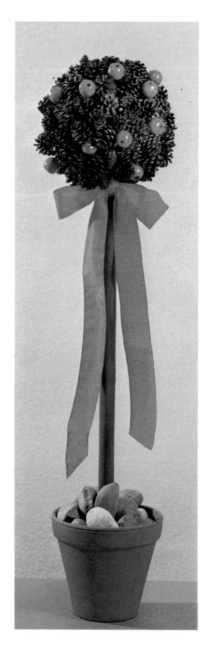

Pine-cone tree supported in a weighted plant pot.

Opposite (top): *Fir-cone centerpiece.*

Opposite (below): *Two small fir-cone pyramids.*

Sharpening the ends of fir sprigs.

Left: *Inserting a wired candle into a plastic-foam pyramid before adding the rest of the decorations.*

Curled wood pyramids

The basic construction of the pyramid with red fruits above, right, is shown on the left of the photograph. To make this you will need a raffia mat for the base, a rectangular piece of wood 20 × 20 × 325mm (¾ × ¾ × 13in.) and four pieces of wood 20 × 20 × 120mm (¾ × ¾ × 4¾in.), together with some rolls of wood shavings 20mm (¾in.) wide which can be bought from a crafts shop, or which you can make yourself by carefully planing a wooden plank.

The four shorter pieces of wood, which form the base of the pyramids, are glued to the raffia mat in a cross formation, leaving a gap at the center to support the upright. Cut up varying lengths of wood shaving to make rings of all sizes and glue or staple them together as shown. Cover the outer rings with red ribbon before

attaching each one to the upright piece of wood.

Wire the beech nuts with red beads in their centers, and cut short lengths of ruscus. Cut some florist's foam into four 325mm (13in.) lengths and press each piece into one of the four corners of the wooden upright, fastening it in position with wire threaded through the innermost rings of wood shaving.

Add the ruscus on either side of the florist's foam so that it partly covers the sides of the rings, and attach a few longer sprigs at the bottom so that the mat is covered. Place wired beech nuts, berries and small fruits down the center of the ruscus sprays and add a few red everlasting flowers at the foot. You can also add small bows of red ribbon at the top if you feel extra embellishment is required.

Above: *Miniature Christmas tree arrangement in a
pottery dish.*

Flowering tree

Another fanciful tree (page 18, right)—this time
a flowering variety which will make a colorful
addition to any part of the home at any time of
year. You will need a strong bowl or pot suitable
for holding the heavy stones or gravel, a natural
weathered branch, and a plastic foam ball.

Use florist's foam or modeling clay together
with gravel and stones to make a strong support
for the branch. Thread a long wire through the
plastic foam ball, after making a hole in it with
a knitting needle, to enable it to be fastened
securely to the branch. The flowers used in this
tree are red ruscus, white everlasting flowers,
golden thistles, red milfoil, yarrow, green scabious, plane-cones, red fruit and berries, and tree
fungus. Any plant materials which do not have
sufficiently long stems should first be wired before inserting them in the plastic foam ball.

Centerpiece in red and gold

The arrangement above needs very few materials. These are two long, red candles, holly branches, orange and red varnished apples or other fruits, green scabious, three gilded elephant ears and hazel twigs.

Attach some florist's foam or non-hardening modeling clay to a small plate or dish—a plain one will do, since it should not be visible when the arrangement is complete. Put the wired candles in the middle and arrange the holly around them. The fruits are positioned between the candles and the elephant ears, with the hazel twigs and scabious added at the outside.

Above: *A flowering tree made from a naturally weathered branch and a decorated plastic-foam ball.*

Gathering wiring ribbon to make a decorative bow.

Ornamental hanging ball

The ball above makes an unusual ceiling decoration. The foundation is a plastic foam ball into which have been wired Wellingtonia or similar cones, yellow ruscus, blue statice, gold-painted beech nuts and yellow varnished pears. Also interspersed are some flowers cut from a gold foil, which can be found on the tops of some beer and fruit juice bottles. These flower petals have been individually cut and wired together with an imitation pearl at their center. Push a long wire through the center of the ball after using a knitting needle to make the hole. Fasten a pine-cone at one end of the wire, and a small hook at the other for hanging, and lastly, conceal the wire with blue ribbon.

A cone and apple hanging.

Curled wood wall-hanging.

Cone and apple hanging

Another decoration for hanging from the ceiling or against a wall appears above, left. This piece needs Weymouth or white pine-cones for the full effect, but any open cones will do. You will need strong hemp or similar rope to carry the clumps of cones. Knot the rope at each point where you intend to hang a bunch of cones. Wire up each cone individually. You will need 12 to 15 cones for half a clump. Each clump is wired up as half; all the wires are twisted together; and then the two half-bundles are brought together by wiring

above the knots in each case. You can hang lacquered apples or berries from the cones, or decorate the intervening rope with ribbon or leaves if you wish.

Curled wood wall hanging

The colorful wall hanging above *(right)* is constructed on a piece of wood 20 × 450mm (¾in. × 18in.). Each circular decoration is made

*A wall flower garland constructed around a straw
wreath.*

from a single length of wood-shaving which has
first been softened in water and then formed into
rings of varying sizes. As each new ring is added,
a little glue is applied and a paper clip is used to
hold the construction together until the glue is
set. All the flowers, fruits and cones have been
attached to the central wooden strip by wire and
short nails.

Flower wall garland

A straw wreath is the foundation of the fruit and
flower wall garland above. The wreath is covered
with moss before the other decorations are
added, after each has been wired. Strong wires
are attached to the wreath for hanging, but they
can be concealed by an attractively tied ribbon.

Pine branch centerpiece

The classical elegance of the long blue arrangement above is perfect for a formal table setting. Its base is a plastic foam mat covered with moss. with a pine branch laid to cover the entire length. The rings are made by stringing together alternate blue and white beads, which, together with bleached cones, varnished apples, berries and dried flowers, are scattered among the pine twigs. The four blue candles are wired firmly in position, and to complete the displays, bows of blue ribbon are knotted around several pine twigs.

Candles

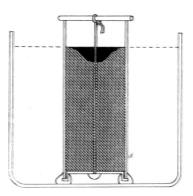

A well begins to form in the wax as the candle cools.

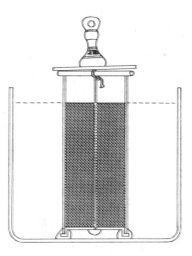

A weight on top of the immersed mold to prevent it from toppling over.

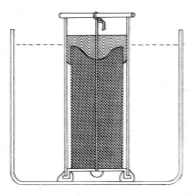

A difficult wedge forms if the well is topped up above the original level of the candle.

Page 23: Multi-layered candles made by pouring different-colored waxes into a mold at different times.

Candles first evolved thousands of years ago and were used as a source of light. Today they are used mainly for decoration. Colored and attractive candles are expensive to buy. Plain candles are cheaper, but not very exciting to look at. It is very easy to make decorative candles yourself, to your own design, size and satisfaction. First you will need the materials and then you will need to know how to use them.

Basic material for making candles

Paraffin wax
Stearin
Wax dyes
Wicks (in various sizes)
Thermometer (cooking type as other kinds will break)
Various pans and/or double boiler
Oil-soluble perfumes (only if you wish to give your candles a perfume)
Mold seal (or non-hardening modeling clay)

The most frequently used paraffin wax is one with a melting temperature of 56°–58°C (133°–136°F), although waxes with higher and lower melting temperatures can also be used to give special effects. Paraffin wax is usually white or cream in color and can be bought either in block or powder form. Always read the maker's instructions so that you know the melting temperature of the wax you have.

Wax dyes are the best coloring agent for paraffin wax and should be used as described in the maker's instructions.

Stearin is a white, flaky, non-corrosive and non-toxic material. Most dyes should be dissolved in a small amount of heated stearin before being added to the paraffin wax, to make sure of full richness of color. The mixture proportions should be about one part stearin to ten parts wax. Stearin also makes the candle opaque, and causes the wax mixture to shrink slightly when cooling thus helping to release the candle from its mold.

The stearin must be melted in a separate saucepan, and the manufacturer's recommended quantity of dye sprinkled or scraped on to it. This mixture should be heated and stirred gently until all the dye has dissolved into a colored liquid and there are no dye particles left on the base of the pan. Then it should be added to molten paraffin wax. Heat the candle wax to pouring temperature, about 82°C (180°F), and transfer it to a warmed jug for easier pouring.

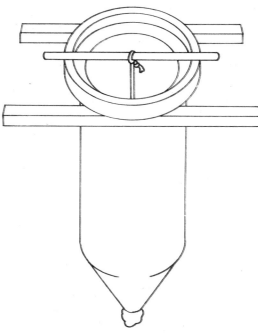

A mold being supported by an improvised rack. After the wick has been threaded through the mold it is tied to a rod at the bottom end, pulled tight, and sealed at the top end with mold seal.

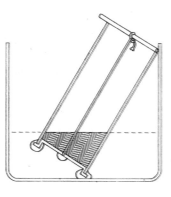

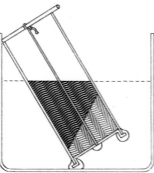

The method for making multi-layered candles by standing the mold at different angles to cool after pouring wax of varying colors.

Remember that wax should *never* be heated over a fierce flame. Asbestos mats will help to disperse direct heat when using gas or open flames. A double boiler is ideal for melting wax, but an ordinary saucepan will do, providing the heat is not too intense.

Use a thermometer that has a range of up to 204°C (400°F). *Never* leave a thermometer in wax that is setting, and don't try to pick set wax off a thermometer to clean it, as this will cause it to break. Clean it by dipping in hot water.

Oil-soluble perfume (*not* alcohol-based) can be added at the last possible moment in the making process. Perfumes are best used sparingly so that they give a delicate aroma rather than a full-bodied smell.

The size of wick used must be related to the height and breadth of the candle. As a general rule, the bigger the candle, the thicker the wick. If the wick is too thin, the wax will melt faster than it can burn and will probably flood the candle; too thick, and there will be insufficient fuel for it, and the wick will burn itself into a smoky flame.

Pouring

Several different kinds of ready-made candle molds, usually made of rubber, can be obtained from crafts shops. But many household containers, such as squeezy bottles, milk cartons, cans, yoghurt cartons and food jars, can be used as molds to make excellent candles. Remember that with every mold, the candle must be able to be released easily when the wax has set.

When using a rubber mold, first choose a wick suitable for the diameter of the candle. Dip the wick in hot wax and pull it straight. Thread the wick through the mold with a special wicking needle, or any needle with a large eye, making sure that the wick is centered in the mold. Tie the bottom end to a rod or stick, pull the top end tight, and seal it with mold seal (or any substance, like non-hardening modeling clay that is leak-proof). Take care not to get any mold seal on the wick. Support the mold by hanging it from an improvised rack (see diagram), or support it between two pieces of wood, allowing the air to circulate around it.

To lengthen the life of rubber molds, use a minimal amount of stearin when dissolving the dye—only about 1 per cent stearin to the wax instead of the usual 10 per cent. Pour the colored wax at 82°C (180°F), saving some for topping up. Tap the side of the mold lightly to remove

trapped air bubbles. Leave until a well forms, and then break the sunken surface with a stick. This will prevent the cooling and contracting wax from distorting the mold. Pour on more hot wax, and repeat this until the surface is flat. If the mold sags, it can easily be reshaped by careful manipulation while it is still warm. When the mold is full, leave it until it is cold. Damage to the candle may result if you try to remove the candle from the mold while it is still warm. To release it, rub the surface of the mold with soapy hands and warm water. Peel it off carefully, and restore the mold to its original shape. Wash and dry it thoroughly and store away from heat and sunlight.

The matt candle surface can be polished by rubbing it with your hands or a soft cloth. A small amount of beeswax in the original candle mixture will make this much easier. Relief work can be highlighted by coloring it with water-soluble paint mixed with a little soap, but do not use too much paint as it will not burn and may clog the wick.

The multi-layered candles on page 23 are made by pouring a variety of colored waxes into a mold at different times. A layer of wax is poured at 82°C (180°F) and allowed to cool until the surface is rubbery. The next color is then poured gently on to the first, at the same temperature as before, and is left to set to the same rubbery surface. The layers are thus built up, and the candle is finally topped up when the well in the center has appeared. By simply standing the mold at an angle, layers can be built up diagonally (see diagram).

Dipping—the oldest method of candlemaking

The great advantage of dipping is that it involves very little pouring. All you need is a pot or jug a little taller than the required height of the candle. Fill the pot with undyed wax and heat it. Tie a length of wick to a stick and dip this into the paraffin wax heated to 82°C (180°F). Then take it out of the wax and wait for 30 seconds, this being the time it takes for each coat of wax to harden. Repeat this process until the candle is as thick as you want it. Hang the finished candles to cool. If you want the candles to be white and straight, simply let them harden off, cut the wick from the stick, and trim neatly.

An economical method for coloring white candles is to float a 50mm (2in.) layer of colored molten candle wax on water that has been heated

Three straight white candles being dipped simultaneously.

to 82°C (180°F). Remember to leave some space at the top of the container because the candle to be dipped will displace some of the water. If a scum forms it can easily be spooned off. The white candle is dipped through the candle wax into the water, and then pulled out. It collects color on the way in and on the way out. If the wax is too hot, hardly any color will be picked up. If the wax is too cool, the candle will be scaly and flaky. Continue the dipping process until the required depth of color is achieved.

Pear-shaped candles

This is a variation of the dipping process. By dipping progressively less of the candle into the wax, a roughly pear-shaped candle will be formed and this should be gently molded by hand between each dipping until it is smooth. A final coat of color can be added in the usual way.

Metal molds

Metal molds can be bought ready-made. They are specially useful because they allow the candle to cool rapidly, and because they have a smooth interior surface, leaving little finishing off to be done.

Make sure the inside of the mold is clean; wax the wick and secure it to a piece of stick. Thread the other end of the wick through the mold base, pull taut, and seal with mold seal. Pour the prepared, colored candle wax into the mold at 88°C (190°F). Let the mold stand for a minute to allow air bubbles to rise, and lightly tap the mold to help them along. Rapid cooling in a water bath will produce a good finish. A bucket filled with cold water will serve as a cooling bath, but remember that the water level should be the same

as the wax level, so first immerse the empty mold to ensure the correct water level. Do not pour wax into a mold that is already in a cooling bath—this will produce unsightly scales.

When all the air bubbles have risen and the mold is hot, lower it carefully into the cooling bath, making sure that no water enters the mold. You may have to weight the top of the mold to prevent it toppling over (diagram page 24). Let the candle cool, until a well in the center begins to form. Break the surface skin and top up at 93°C (200°F), taking care not to overfill above the original level, as this will cause a wedge to form and it will be very difficult to release the candle from the mold (diagram page 24). Allow the candle to cool, invert the mold, and slide the candle out. Trim the wick and level the base.

If you are making your own mold and using a container with a fixed base, or one through which you cannot bore a hole, then the wick must be inserted after the candle is set. You can do this by first drilling a hole with an ordinary thin hand-drill, and then threading the waxed wick into the candle, and topping up with hot wax. Alternatively, you can insert a knitting needle or skewer down the center of the candle while it is still soft. Pull it out once the wax has almost set, and then insert the wick.

A dipped candle where several layers of different colors, each about 6mm (¼in.) thick, have been added. When the candle has hardened completely it is carved back to reveal the brilliant colors within.

The bunch of grapes was made by pouring candle wax into refrigerator ice trays and fastening the bunch round a wick.

Colored chunks of wax stuck on the outside of two white candles. Pour a thin sheet of strongly dyed wax into a tray and let it harden.
When set, break or carve it into pieces. Press a hot knife blade on to the surface of the candle, and place a piece of wax on the blade. Slide the knife away, welding the two wax surfaces together.

A candle made with a rubber mold, on which relief work had been highlighted by coloring with a water-soluble paint.

How to secure the wick in an improvised mold with an open end.

Plaited candles

When several colors are required for dipped candles, cut the same number of lengths of plastic drain pipe and put them in a bucket containing hot water. Float different-colored molten waxes in each piece of drain pipe and maintain the temperature at 82°C (180°F). By dipping basic white candles in rotation, several colored candles can be made at once.

When the candles are the right color, and the outer surfaces have dried, they can be plaited together. This is much easier to do if you have someone to hold the candles at one end. If the candles harden before plaiting is complete, return each to its respective color, and dip a few times until it becomes soft again.

Candlesticks

Metal foil candlesticks

These are made from double-sided metal foil, which is usually sold by the roll in stores that sell gift-wrapping paper. Draw the lines shown in the pattern very carefully. The folding will be made much easier if all the lines are marked with a hard pencil, as then they will be visible on the other side of the foil.

In the diagrams, all heavy lines indicate edges that stand out, and thin lines indicate edges that lie back.

To make the gold candlestick, the strip of foil should be 90mm (3½in.) wide and 420mm (16½in.) long. The pattern in which this should be folded is given below left. Mark three zigzag lines, the center line on the front and the other two on the back of the foil. The center line is folded to the front, the others towards the back.

To make the blue candlestick you will need a strip of paper 85mm (3in.) wide and 480mm (19in.) long. Draw the three zigzag lines as shown in the second diagram below: the middle line on the front and the other two on the back. Fold the accordion-like pleats in both directions first, and then the center zigzag toward the front and the others toward the back.

Since these candlesticks are very light, it is best to set the candle firmly on a cardboard or metal holder which can be concealed under the paper-holder.

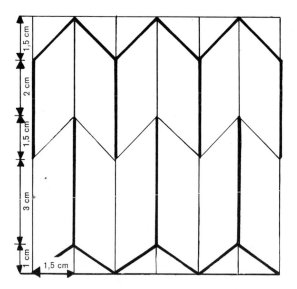

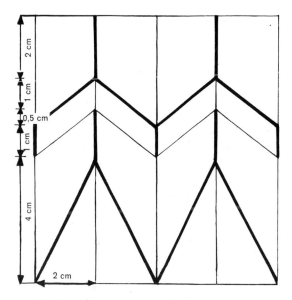

Opposite: *Candlesticks made from colored metal foil. Diagrams and folding patterns are shown above, those for the gold candlestick on the left, those for the blue candlestick on the right.*

Top: *Flower candlestick.* Right: *Cross candlestick.*
Left: *Spiral candlestick.*
*When spirals have been shaped, glue them with
woodworking adhesive while they are still damp,
and clamp them in position using clothes pegs (pins)
or paperclips.*

Curled wood candlesticks

These are made from thick, curly wood-shavings.
They can be bought from craft shops or you can
make them yourself if you plane a plank of wood
carefully. The shavings come in a variety of different spirals, and larger spirals can be made by
very carefully uncoiling smaller ones. Real
wood-shavings are only suitable for making
small decorations. To make larger items, you will
need chipwood (veneer edging) strips which are
sold in rolls from a craft supplier and range in
width from 10mm (³/₈in.) to 45mm (1³/₄in.).

These are much thicker and stronger than
wood-shavings but need to be soaked in warm
water for 10 minutes before use, as they are not
so elastic and break easily if stressed. Once
shaped, glue them with wood-working adhesive
while still damp and clamp with a clothes pin.

Flower candlestick

You need one wooden wheel 30mm (1¼in.) diameter, one wooden wheel 40mm (1½in.) diameter and assorted wood-shavings. The flower
shape is made simply by gluing the ends of chipwood (edging) loops in between the two wooden
disks. Once you have decided how large each
loop-shaped petal is to be, measure off eight
equal loops and glue them to the lower wheel.
Glue smaller loops inside the large ones and
when set, glue the two wheels together and drive

Christmas table centerpiece.

a thin screw through both of them on to which the candle is attached. Lastly, add eight smaller spirals to enhance the design.

Cross candlestick

Join two thin and narrow 150mm (6in.) long pieces of wood in the shape of a cross. Cut a notch in the center of each and interlock them. Glue a small wooden disk in the center and then fill in the spaces between the arms with varying chipwood (veneer edging) spirals, formed round small wooden disks. Decorate the ends of the cross with small wood-shaving spirals.

Spiral candlestick

Pierce a small wooden wheel with a screw to hold a candle. Glue one end of a long chipwood strip to the wheel and coil it round to make three rings. Fill in the rings with small spirals and glue the end of the long chipwood (veneer edging) strip to the middle ring. To make it more sturdy, glue a cardboard disk underneath.

Christmas table centerpiece

To make this delightful table decoration, you need: 2 thin pieces of wood 500mm (20in.) long, 4 thin pieces of wood 170mm (6½in.) long, 1

wooden wheel 60mm (2½in.) diameter, 4 wooden wheels 30mm (1¼in.) diameter, 16 disks cut from 15mm (½in.) dowel, 16 flat toothpicks, 4 cardboard disks 40mm (1½in.) diameter, assorted chipwood (veneer edging) and woodshavings, 4 red candles, gloss paint and wood-working adhesive.

Start by gluing the two longer pieces of wood together to form a cross. Even out the levels at the center where the two pieces cross by gluing on 20mm (¾in.) offcuts of the same wood. Paint all the wooden wheels and disks gold, and when dry glue the largest one to the center of the cross. Make four smaller crosses by gluing on the shorter pieces of wood and then glue on a cardboard disk at the center of each cross. Paint all the crosses red.

Glue on to each cardboard disk four of the flat toothpicks and eight chipwood (edging) strips 75mm (3in.) long with a V cut in the end as shown. In the center of each disk glue on a wooden wheel with a nail through it, and eight chipwood (edging) spirals. Decorate the ends of each cross with 16 small wood disks and wood shavings, protecting them from wax drips with clear plastic circles on each nail.

The trunk of the tree in the center is a piece of wood 250mm (10in.) long and 15mm (½in.) square, shaved to a point at the top. Join it to a small wooden wheel and to the center of the cross. Then build up the foliage with chipwood (edging) spirals, starting from the bottom, and be careful not to make the tree too wide or the wood shavings will touch the candles. Fill in the gaps between the main spirals with smaller shavings.

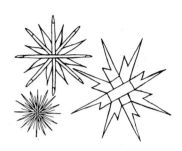

Stars

Page 35. *A delicate eightfold star made from two fourfold stars, one in straw and the other in grass.*

1. *The face of a simple star.*
2. *The back of the same simple star.*
3. *A twofold star (two simple stars joined together). Each of the two simple stars has been made with a different straw.*

4–6. *Three examples of fourfold stars (each made from a pair of twofold stars), using a combination of different straws and grasses.*

7. *A combination of straw and grass.*
8. *An eightfold star with all spokes trimmed to an equal length.*
9. *Two fourfold stars with spokes of contrasting lengths and trimmed points, joined to form an eightfold star.*

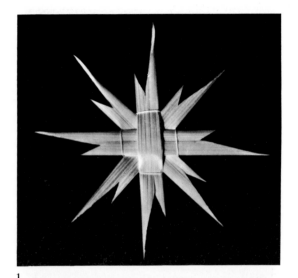

1

2

3

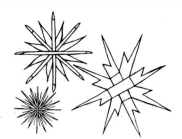

4

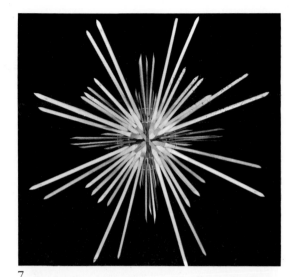

7

5

8

6

9

This star uses the one shown on page 35 as its starting point. Each of the double stars has one point which is twice as long as the others and this is inserted into the appropriate points of the central star. The grass star has 16 extra-long points to carry the outer wreath of double stars.

Delicate, satiny straws and grasses make truly lovely ornaments for Christmas and can also be used as wall decorations all the year round.

The possibilities for inventing new designs are virtually without limit, and once you have mastered the techniques for making the straw stars illustrated here, you will be able to construct designs of your own.

Do not expect to be able to create complicated ornaments at the very beginning. These take a little more patience, so begin by making a number of simple stars.

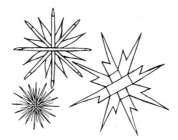

You will need scissors, medium-weight unbleached thread, and a supply of straw and grass. Country-dwellers may be able to collect these from fields near where they live, otherwise they can be obtained from a handicrafts supplier. The straw must be soaked thoroughly in hot water before you begin working, or it will split and crack. If you need longer lengths of grass or straw, you can join two short lengths together by inserting one into another.

The stars illustrated on page 36 are the basic structure on which all other stars are formed. To make the first star, take four straws of equal length: 50–75 mm (2–3 in.) is a convenient size to begin with. Place two straws together to form a cross, the other two to form an 'x', and then join the two. The first photograph shows the face, the second photograph the back of a simple star. Study these two photographs carefully to see the exact position of each of the straws. Bind the star with thread, alternating over one straw, under the next, over the third, and so on. You must be careful not to have the thread too loose, or the star will quickly lose its shape. On the other hand, if you have it too tight, the straw will be crushed.

Make a number of simple stars, experimenting with various ways of cutting the points. When you are able to construct a simple star that looks elegant, neat and well made, you are ready to go on to more complex stars.

Photograph 3 on page 36 shows a two-fold star made of eight straws of equal length, and is basically composed of two simple stars. Join pairs of straws in the following sequence: cross, 'x', cross, 'x'. An alternative method is to form a cross with two straws and then simply add the remaining six straws in a spiral configuration. Bind off with thread, over, under, over, and so on, as for the simple star. You will notice from the photographs and from your own work that the thread is always brought *over* the straws that lie on the top, and *under* the straws that lie on the bottom.

The same photograph (page 36, no. 3) also shows the effect of using a variety of materials. The wide upper portion of the straw is used for one of the simple stars and the hollow lower portion for the other.

The three photographs 4–6 on page 37 show examples of fourfold stars, each constructed from a pair of twofold stars. Use a combination of grass or thin hollow straw and wider straw (for example, one twofold star of grass and one of straw), since there will be 16 straws overlapping at the center. Always keep to the sequence described for the simple and twofold stars.

A pair of sharp, straight scissors at least 100mm (4in.) long is required for trimming the straw to a clean point. The photographs show a variety of ways of cutting the points. The large star on page 38 is an eightfold star made of straw and grass. Make sure when constructing stars like this that grass and straw points alternate as you join the spokes, and remember that simple stars are the basis of all the examples shown. A simple star is generally made *only* of straw or *only* of grass; the combinations are achieved by using the two types together.

The star on page 38 uses the large star on page 35 as its starting point. In this example, however, the grass star has 16 extra-long points which serve to carry an outer wreath of double stars. Each of the double stars has one point which is twice as long as the others, and this is inserted into the appropriate points of the central star.

Photograph no. 7 on page 37 shows a combination of straw and grass; photograph no. 8 shows an eightfold star made of two fourfold stars with the straws all trimmed to an equal length; and photograph no. 9 shows two more fourfold stars with contrasting lengths and trimmed points, joined to form an eightfold star.

Metal foil stars

As a contrast to the natural materials used for making straw stars, why not make spectacular, shimmering stars from metal foil? Foil can be obtained from crafts shops, but make sure that you buy the heavyweight, double-sided kind, preferably with a different color on each side.

For the simplest kind of star, fold a narrow strip of foil (the wider, the longer) into accordion pleats 12–25mm (½–1in.) wide. Trim top and bottom evenly, and cut away portions from the right and left as shown in the diagram below. Finally, join the ends of the strip, and gather the lower edge with thread.

To make the simplest metal foil star, trim away the shaded portions of an accordion-pleated narrow strip of foil, join the ends of the strip, and gather the lower edge with thread.

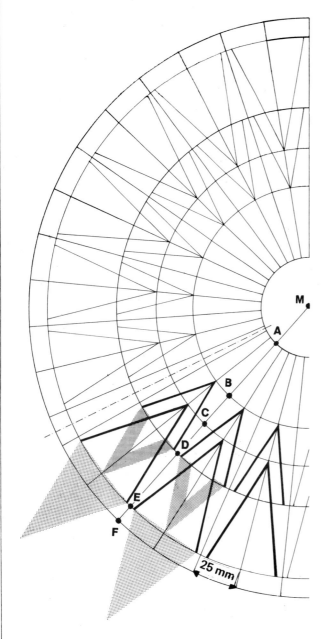

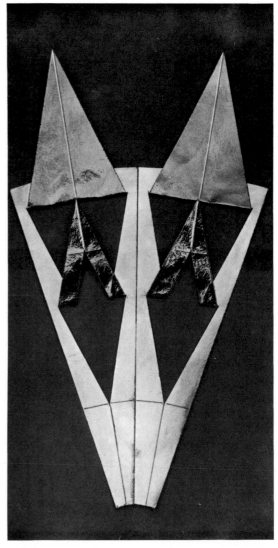

Cutting and folding patterns for the large blue and gold foil star on page 41.
Measurements:
M—A = 25mm
M—B = 65mm
M—C = 85mm
M—D = 105mm
M—E = 145mm
M—F = 155mm

The two large ornamental stars illustrated on pages 41 and 43 can be made as follows. Using a pencil and ruler, carefully draw the lines along which the foil is to be folded. After you have drawn all the lines from the pattern provided, crease all the vertical folds twice, forward and backward, to make all further folding easier. Unless otherwise indicated, all heavy lines on the diagrams mark folds to be made to the front of your star. Heavy zigzag lines should be drawn on the reverse side of the foil. Thin zigzag lines should be drawn on the front of the foil. Since you are working with double-sided foil, any line you draw on one side will also be visible on the other, which makes folding much easier. If you use a pencil with a hard lead, and apply some pressure (not too much, or the foil will tear), you will have a very clear guideline. For this reason,

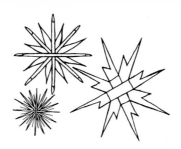

A large ornamental star made from a circle of foil which is then folded like a fan. Use the pattern on page 40 to cut and measure the double-sided foil.

you must mark (on the side indicated) only those lines along which you will actually fold, and draw all supplementary guidelines very lightly.

The ornamental star above is folded like a fan. The foil we have used is gold on the front and brilliant blue on the back. Instead of working with a strip of foil, as in the first, simple example, use a circle as the basic shape. This speeds up the construction process, and also, since the rays at the center taper down, the star will be flatter.

Draw six circles, A, B, C, D, E, and F, around the center M. The radii of the various circles are listed opposite. To mark the segments on circle F, a compass is most useful. Now draw all the lines from M to the points on circle F. Cut away the smallest circle A. Using a sharp craft knife, cut along the heavy zigzag lines, making sure that you do not cut beyond the lines, or the points will fall away. When all the points have been cut, fold them down as indicated by the shaded area in the diagram, and open out the circle. Fold the star in such a way that the

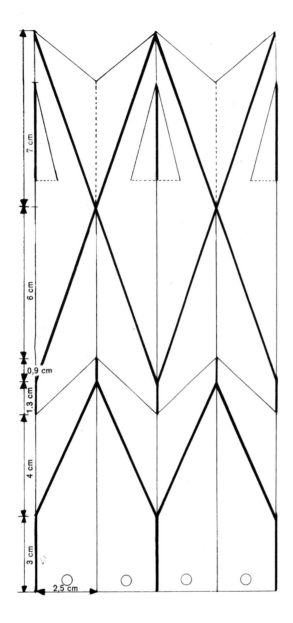

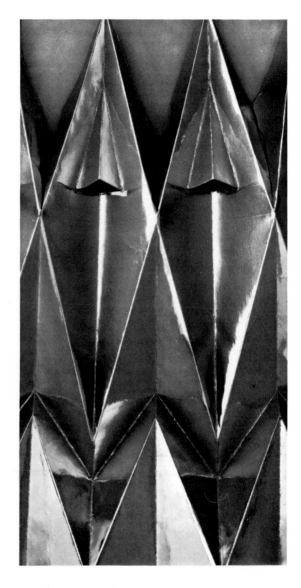

How to fold the foil in order to make the ornamental star shown on page 43.

folded-down pleats come to lie face down as shown in the black and white photograph. Since the original circle will not allow for all this folding in, insert another quarter-circle, folded in the same way.

To make the ornamental star on the next page, you will need a strip of foil 1m (40in.) long and 220mm (8⅝in.) wide. Follow the diagram above to make the guidelines: vertical lines 25mm (1in.) apart for the accordion pleats, four zigzag lines for folding and one, at the top, for cutting. As before, draw the heavy lines on the back, the light ones on the front of your foil. After folding the accordion pleats in both directions to make

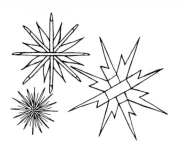

subsequent folding easier, fold the second (light line) zigzag toward the front, and the first, third and fourth (heavy line) zigzags toward the back. Cut along the base of each triangle, indicated by dotted lines, and fold the small triangles inward. Cut out the points at the top, as shown in the diagram, and cut in along the vertical dotted lines. Bend the flaps just formed toward the back, and glue them together. Finally, join the two ends of the strip and gather the lower edge with thread until the star is formed.

An ornamental star, this time made from a strip of double-sided metal foil 1·3m (50in.) long and 220mm (8⅝in.) wide. Make guidelines following the pattern shown on page 42.

Christmas tree ornaments

Decorating the Christmas tree is a traditional part of the Christmas festivities and gives pleasure to grown-ups and children alike. Ornaments for the tree can be very expensive, so why not make your own, following the suggestions given here? Further ideas for Christmas tree ornaments can also be found in the chapters on Stars, Angels, and Paper Chains.

Ornamental balls

The decorations on these and the following three pages are all made from white polystyrene balls which can be obtained from crafts and model shops. Each ball has a slight ridge around the middle, which is a useful design aid as you can draw pencil lines on the ball parallel to the ridge and equidistant from it. Before drawing the decorative pattern on the ball, give it two or three coats of water-based paint. You will find it easier to paint if you pierce the ball with a thin knitting needle to hold it fast. (Stick the other end of the needle in a base of non-hardening modeling clay.) Allow the ball to dry thoroughly before proceeding with the design.

To divide a ball into a number of equal-sized areas for painting, measure the diameter by placing a narrow strip of paper around the center. Fold the paper in two, then four, then eight and mark the points of the folds in pencil. You can then use the paper to divide the ball into halves, quarters, and so on.

Use fine-pointed brushes to paint the designs; a flat one is best for the base coat and large areas or stripes. To make a hanger for the balls, bend a piece of florist's wire about 20mm (¾in.) long into a U-shape with tweezers, and stick the ends into the ball. For gluing, use a polystyrene glue or latex adhesive.

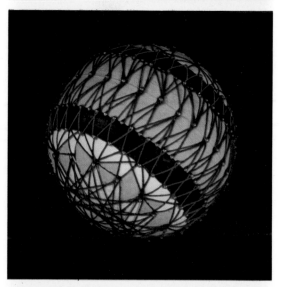

To make the thread-decorated balls on this page you will need poster or emulsion (tempera) paints for applying the base color; pins, ordinary or glass-headed; and thread in various colors.

This page: *Three thread-decorated balls. The broad color stripes were painted before threading, but the small triangles and diamonds were added after threading with a selection of colored threads.*

Opposite: *You can include gaily decorated painted balls in an arrangement of flowers, trees and branches. Here the balls have been hung from suspended branches complete with berries and cones.*

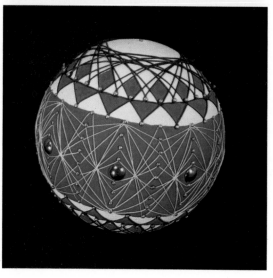

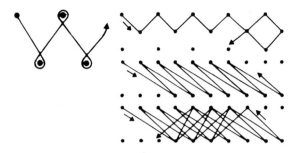

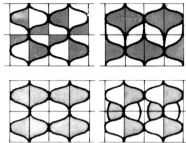

Above: *The method for threading the pins to create different patterns.*

Above: *Four alternative methods of coloring the same pattern for decorated ornamental balls.*

Right: *Choose toning when decorating a tree, although you can use different patterns. Those on the tree, and on the pine–cone branch (left), are all based on the onion-shape pattern shown at the top of the page (right).*

Above: *A conifer branch wired to a gnarled tree root with chains attached for suspending from the ceiling. Hang painted balls from the branches with thread, and fix the candles on the ends of long nails driven through the wood.*

Divide the central ridge on the ball into equal segments using a narrow strip of paper as already described. Build up the foundation for the pattern by sticking pins along the central ridge, and in further rows parallel to it. Allow the heads to stick up about 3mm (⅛in.) from the surface so that the thread can be wound under them. Begin and end by knotting the thread to one of the pins.

For the basic zigzag decoration, work as shown in the top left diagram, page 46, right around the ball, between two rows of pins. Changing the direction of the thread on the next round will create a diamond pattern. All kinds of beautiful patterns can be created by varying the pin spacing and the direction of the threading. More pins can be inserted during threading to vary the pattern, but it is generally better to use fewer pins and allow them to carry as much threading as possible.

Once the threading is complete, push the pins home into the ball. You can now pick out some of the triangle and diamond shapes with paint as we have done. Broad stripes and other large areas of color should be painted before you start threading.

Metal foil ornaments

The beautiful metal foil decorations shown on the following pages are all made from heavyweight double-sided metal foil, which can be obtained from crafts shops.

Use a pencil and ruler to copy the diagrams

Above: *The three stylized Christmas tree shapes used for these mobiles are 275mm (11in.) high and 200mm (8in.) wide cut from thin plywood. Holes 115mm (4½in.) diameter have been cut out of the wood and 100mm (4in.) diameter painted polystyrene balls hang in the holes. A small hole was drilled at the tree's uppermost point for the hanging thread, and the threads for hanging the balls were painted green and glued to the wood.*

very carefully on to your foil and draw the lines along which you will fold the foil. Crease all the vertical folds twice, forward and backward, to make all further folding easier. All heavy lines in the diagrams indicate folds which should be made to the front. Zigzag lines should be drawn on the reverse side of the foil. Since you are working with two-sided foil, any line you draw on one side will also be visible on the other. Use a pencil with a hard lead, but do not apply too much pressure or the foil will tear.

To make the red ornament on the opposite page, follow the diagram top left on page 50. You will need a strip of foil 600mm (24in.) long and 150mm (6in.) wide. Ignore the fine dotted lines, which are part of the variation for making the gold ornament.

The accordion-type folds are 25mm (1in.) wide, and the zigzag lines should be drawn on the back of the foil.

Fold the accordion pleats in both directions, and then fold along the light lines toward the front, and heavy lines toward the back, then fold the zigzag lines toward the back. Join the ends

Above: *Four glittering metal foil decorations.*

of the strip and gather at top and bottom with thread.

To make the gold ornament in the center of the photograph, use the dotted guidelines as well. Follow the instructions for the red ornament, and at the end, fold the additional points toward the front.

If you push the zigzag lines together until the points meet you can construct the other gold ornament (shown, top left). Again ignore the dotted lines. Reduce the upper and lower bands to a width of 25mm (1in.). In this case, too, draw the lines on the back of the foil and push the folds toward the front.

To make the green ornament, you will need a strip of green foil 295mm (11¾in.) long and 115mm (4½in.) wide. Make a cardboard tem-

plate from the shape shown in the drawing on page 51, and use it to mark four arches along each edge on the reverse side of the foil. Spaces of 20mm (¾in.) should be left at each end as well as between the arches. Crease the arches inward as shown in the black and white photograph center left page 50, make an overlapping joint of the ends of the strip of green foil, and, without letting it show on the outside curves, draw a thread through all the top and bottom inside curves to give the final shape before hanging.

The easiest way to make the quill stars shown on page 51 is from a number of foil disks, marked in segments as shown in the black and white photograph on page 50 (*top right*). Fold along each of the diameter markings and then

CHRISTMAS CRAFTS

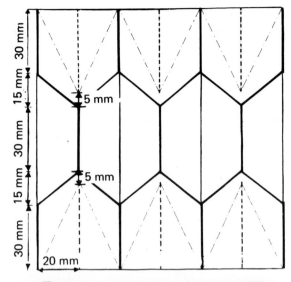

Top left: *Pattern for the gold and red ornaments.*
Center left: *Detail of the folding pattern for the gold center ornament.*

Below left: *Detail of the folded arches for the green ornament.*

One of the foil disks used to make the quill stars illustrated in color on the next page. Mark each foil disk in eight segments, fold along each of the diameters and cut as far as the inner circle. Roll each segment around a pencil point into a cone shape.

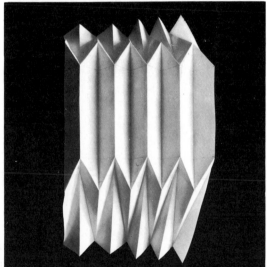

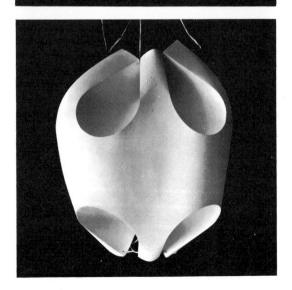

Threading the foil disks after individual segments have been rolled and glued.

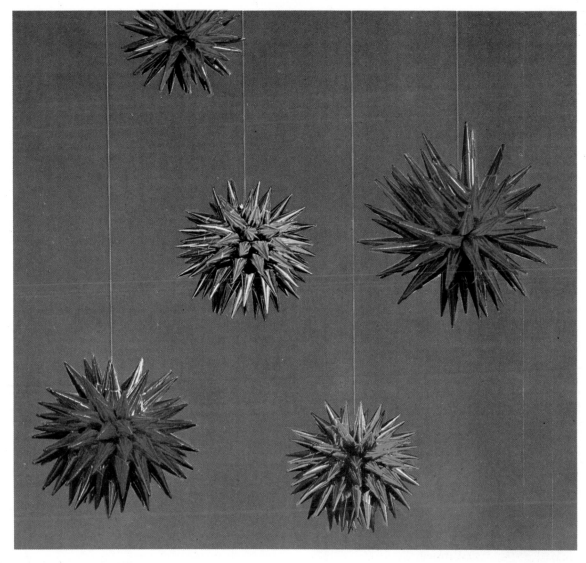

An assortment of quill stars. You can suspend them from the ceiling on various lengths of nylon thread to give the effect shown here, or use them to decorate your tree.

knitting needle into a cone shape and gluing the shape in position. You will need about eight or ten disks with a diameter of 150mm (6in.). The inner circle has a radius of 20mm (¾in.). They are all joined together with a thread through the middle, and the points are arranged to give the quill effect.

Tree-top ornaments

If you have trimmed your tree with stars, angels, garlands and ball ornaments that you have made yourself, you will surely not want to buy a factory-made ornament for the tip of the tree. Instead, you might mount one of the ornaments shown on page 49, or one of the stars shown on pages 41 or 43, on a cone of metal foil.

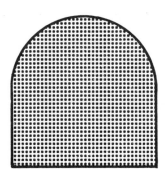

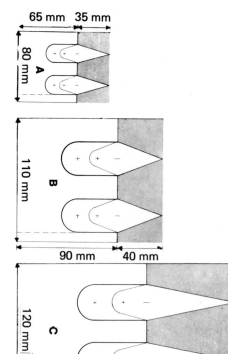

65 mm   35 mm

80 mm

A

+ + −
+ + −

110 mm

B

+ + −
+ + −

90 mm   40 mm

120 mm

C

+ + −
+ + −
+ + −

130 mm   90 mm

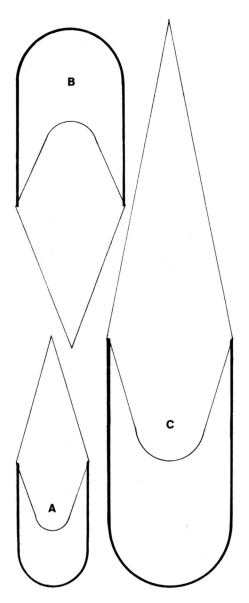

B

A

C

Each of the two stars shown on page 53 is made from a circular piece of foil, using the diagram on page 40, but reducing the diameter of the largest circle to 200mm (8in.) and arranging the folded-out points more simply.

Your tree-top ornament may be mounted on a simple cone, or you may like to fashion a cone which echoes the tip of the tree itself. Work this shape in three separate pieces, cut, folded and glued individually, and then joined according to size. Both the large curve and the smaller one within it now have points on top of them. The three shapes from A (small) to C (large) are shown actual size. B and C shapes are 25mm

Two ornaments for the top of the Christmas tree which have been crowned with metal foil stars. Instructions for the stars appear on pages 39–43. Also illustrated are patterns for the supports, and a black and white photograph showing the method of folding.

(1in.) apart, but *A* shapes are only 20mm (¾in.) apart. In each case, the gluing edge is indicated on the right.

The larger curves are marked off on the reverse side of the foil, the smaller ones on the front. Cut out the shaded areas to make the points. Fold the larger curves from the front inward, and then the smaller ones, together with the points, from the back outward, as shown in the black and white photograph (opposite, bottom left).

Angels

No Christmas would be complete without angels, so in this chapter we show you how to make them in both straw and metal foil.

Straw angels

For the straw angels you will need scissors, thread (medium-weight, unbleached, or in colors). If you live in the country, you may be able to collect your own supply of straw and grass. Otherwise these may be obtained from your local crafts supplier. To avoid splitting and cracking, the straw must always be soaked thoroughly before you begin working.

The diagrams on this page, figs 1–9 together with the numbered instructions below, explain how to make the first angel illustrated on page 56. Details for the other angels and their musical instruments are included later.

1. Make a bundle of 10 thin straws, 175–200mm (7–8in.) long.
2. Tie it tightly by winding three times around with thread, and knot the thread.
3. Trim the tops of the straws to a point.
4. Turn the bundle upside down and bend all the straws downward.
5. Tie again, as shown, to form the head and neck of the angel.
6. Tie a bundle of five straws together at the middle and insert them below the neck as arms, keeping ten 'body' straws in the front and ten in the back.
7. Tie another bundle, this time of seven straws, at the middle and insert into the back as wings. You should now have eight 'body' straws coming over the wings, and two between the wings and arms. The two straws left between wings and arms should be brought downward in such a way that they cover the openings left by inserting the bundles.
8. Tie the waist tightly. Bend the arms downward and tie at the elbows and wrists. Fix the wings in place by interweaving the straws with a length of split straw.
9. Add a short overskirt of 24 very thin straws, tied on at the waist. Conceal the threads at the neck and waist with split straw.

To make the second angel on page 56, spread the sleeve straws and fix in place by interweaving with a length of split straw. Make the overskirt with about 30 straws, having trimmed the bottom end of each with a straw ring. Each of the

An angel with downswept wings about to play a harp.

Below: *Stages of making straw angels.*

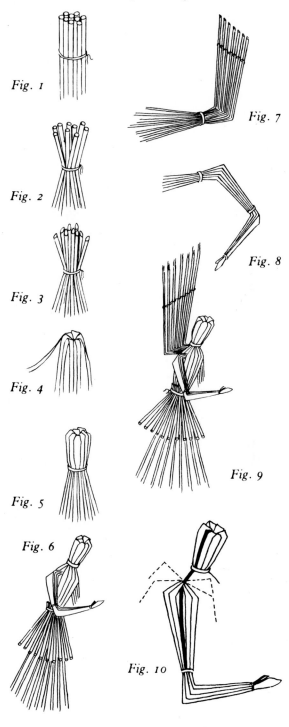

Fig. 1

Fig. 2

Fig. 3

Fig. 4

Fig. 5

Fig. 6

Fig. 7

Fig. 8

Fig. 9

Fig. 10

Fig 10 Tying two crossed straws over one straw from the side of the head.

Left: *An angel made by following the diagrams on page 55.*
Right: *The same angel, but with spread sleeves and overskirt.*

long wings is a separate bundle of nine straws, tied together three times in the middle and inserted as in step 7, on page 55.

To make the downswept wings of the angel playing the harp on page 54 and the angel blowing a woodwind instrument on page 57, choose one straw coming from each side of the head. Over each of these, tie two crossed straws (see

fig. 10). Now gather the five straws of each of the arms, bend at the shoulder, and tie off at the elbows and wrists. For the wings, raise eight straws below the neck in two separate bundles. Bend one straw of each bundle out horizontally, bring the remaining three straws of each bundle a short distance down the back, and then bend upward to a right angle. Re-join the bundles of three to the horizontal straws and add to each a bundle of five additional straws, the tops of which will again form a kind of Elizabethan collar (fig. 11, page 57). Fix the wings in place by interweaving the nine straws of each with a

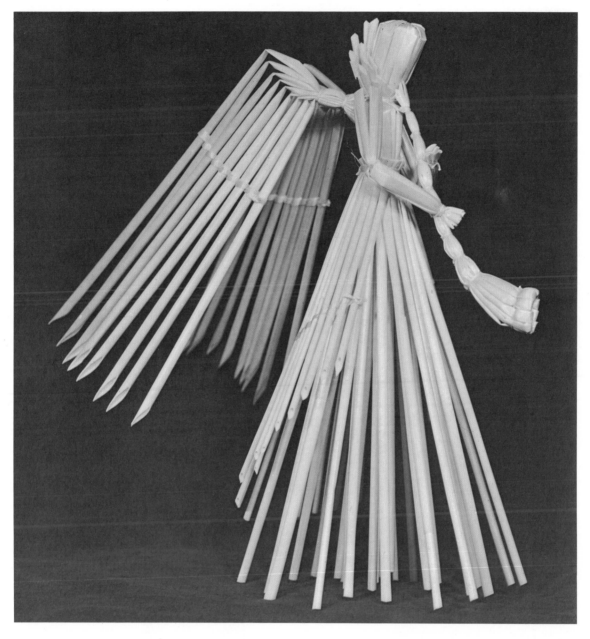

A straw angel with downswept wings, playing a woodwind instrument.

length of split straw. For the overskirt, tie on about 35 thin straws at the waist, interweave with split straws, and trim as shown.

To make the harp, tie nine straws to the base of the upright post, and bend them outward at right angles in groups of three. The strings of split straws are tied to the frame of the harp.

For the woodwind instrument, pull 14 straws half-way through a straw ring, bend the straws in half and arrange them around the ring. Tie

the straws between five and seven times, progressively trimming away some of the straws to achieve the tapered shape.

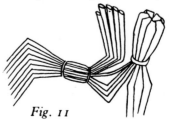

Fig. 11

Above: *The tops of the straws form an Elizabethan collar behind the head.*

Metal foil angels

The photographs on this page, and 60 and 61, show a variety of angel figures made from thick metal foil. Metal foil is easy to work with, and can be bent, folded and painted, as well as printed and embossed. You can give the silver foil any color you wish, while retaining its metal gleam, by using transparent metal colors. You will need only the basic colors of yellow, red and light blue, which you can mix on the silver foil to produce a wide range of colors. For example, a mixture of yellow and blue will give green.

A decorative candle-holder angel with four little doors, one to be opened on each Sunday of Advent.

Thinners or nail-polish removers can be used as cleaners and paint removers, but remember to follow the directions for use. It is especially important to clean your paint brushes after use.

Impress the pattern on the foil first, using a blunt knitting needle or discarded ballpoint pen. The resulting grooves will prevent the painted areas from mixing. If you want a line or pattern to stand out in silver from the colored background, it should be embossed by working from the reverse side of the foil. After you have finished painting, this relief pattern can be wiped with a small rag and a drop of paint remover. Interesting patterns may also be produced by scraping off the paint with a knitting needle.

In their simplest form, each metal foil angel is made from a piece of metal foil cut as a segment of a circle. This segment is then formed into a cone shape and glued. The heads are made from cotton wool (absorbent cotton), paper, polystyrene or wooden balls, depending on the size of the angel. For small angels the head is fastened to a matchstick, around which the dress is then glued.

An angel's head made from a wooden ball screwed to a wine bottle cork.

Pattern for the dress of the Advent candle-holder angel pictured on page 60.

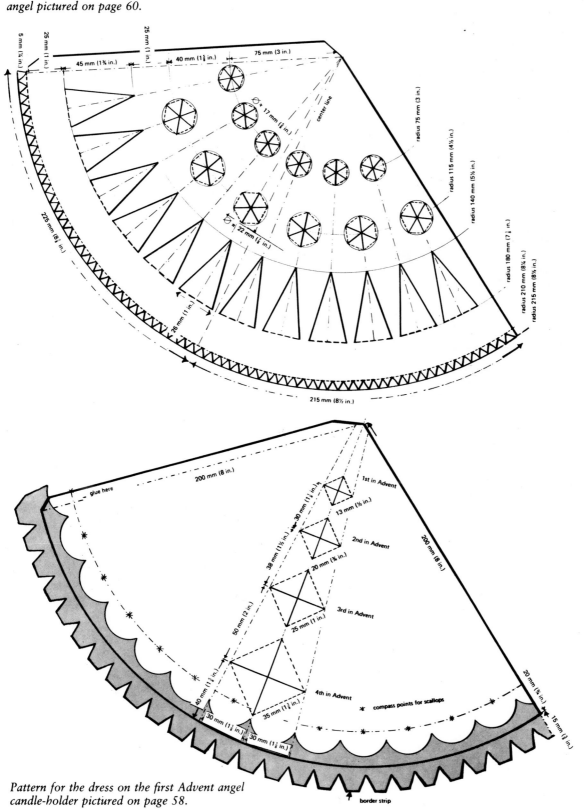

5 mm (¼ in.)
25 mm (1 in.)
25 mm (1 in.)
45 mm (1¾ in.)
40 mm (1½ in.)
75 mm (3 in.)
center line
17 mm (⅔ in.)
22 mm (⅞ in.)
radius 75 mm (3 in.)
radius 115 mm (4½ in.)
radius 140 mm (5½ in.)
radius 180 mm (7⅛ in.)
radius 210 mm (8¼ in.)
radius 215 mm (8½ in.)
225 mm (8¾ in.)
28 mm (1 in.)
215 mm (8½ in.)

Pattern for the dress on the first Advent angel candle-holder pictured on page 58.

glue here
200 mm (8 in.)
1st in Advent
13 mm (½ in.)
30 mm (1¼ in.)
2nd in Advent
38 mm (1½ in.)
20 mm (¾ in.)
200 mm (8 in.)
3rd in Advent
50 mm (2 in.)
25 mm (1 in.)
compass points for scallops
20 mm (¾ in.)
4th in Advent
40 mm (1⅝ in.)
35 mm (1⅜ in.)
15 mm (⅝ in.)
30 mm (1⅛ in.)
30 mm (1⅛ in.)
border strip

59

An Advent angel candle-holder decorated with foliage and dried flowers. Each of the Advent windows displays a different Christmas motif. The windows show best if the angel is placed over a low-power electric light; on no account place it above a candle.

To make a head for a large angel, bore a hole through a wooden ball. The neck is made from a wine bottle cork which has been similarly bored. The cork should be trimmed slightly at the top with a sharp craft knife to make it narrower. Now drive a thin screw 100 mm (4in.) long through both the cork and the ball so that the point sticks out 10mm (⅜in.) at the top. This point is used to fix the candle and should be warmed slightly to make fixing easier. If you do not want to use your angel as a candle-holder, you can stick flowers or other decorations on the head instead; and of course then there is no need for the screw to emerge from the head.

The head and neck should be painted with white or soft pink matt paint. Use a water-based paint for polystyrene balls. Allow the paint to dry thoroughly, then add facial features with a fine-pointed paint brush, or use eyebrow pencils for drawing eyes and nose, and lipstick for rosy cheeks and mouths. Instead of painting the features, you might prefer to use two decorative pins with blue or black glass bead heads for the eyes, or dark-colored sequins held in place with, ordinary pins.

Hair can be made from wool, cotton wool (absorbent cotton), metal foil or dolls' hair, and glued to the head around the screw. To make hair from metal foil, take some strips of foil 50mm (2in.) wide and about the same length. Cut these into very narrow strips and glue them around the face. Wind the strips around a knitting needle or paint brush handle to form the curls.

When the hair is in place, round off or trim the top edge of the cone, glue it together and then glue it to the neck cork, leaving a little of the cork showing to form the neck.

The candle-holder angel on page 58 is made from a white ball 40–50mm (1½–2in.) in diameter, a screw or nail 100mm (4in.) long, a wine bottle cork, thick white drawing paper about 250 × 350mm (10 × 14in.), blue and gold metal foil, blue sequins, eight small pearl or gold beads, one white candle about 20mm (¾in.) in diameter and 70mm (2¾in.) long, and thread and clear adhesive for fixing.

The front of the dress has four little doors, one to be opened on each Sunday of Advent. These are made from gold foil with the numbers 1 to 4 and the decorative borders worked from the back with a knitting needle.

Draw the paper cone shape on the drawing paper, using ruler and compasses and the measurements given in the drawing at the bottom of page 59.

Left: *A very simple angel made from segment-shape silver metal foil for the body and a trimmed segment-shape for her skirt.*
Right: *The angel made from the diagrams on page 62.*

Cut along the crossed lines on each door with a sharp craft knife. Mark, but do not cut, along the dotted door outlines, so that the flaps can be folded outward. Stick the prepared gold foil numbers on the back, and cut out the cone shape.

Lay the paper cone shape on blue metal foil, and draw around the semicircular edge, allowing about 15mm (⅝in.) to turn under. Place a compass on the star markings to draw scallops all along the upper edge of the foil, and cut out. Snip along the lower edge as shown. Glue the scalloped edge to the front of the paper cone, starting in the center. Fold back the turn-under, and glue down firmly.

At the point between each scallop, glue on a blue sequin or a circle of blue foil made with a hole-puncher. (The sequins should be picked up with tweezers, dotted carefully with clear adhesive, and pressed into place with a rag.) Also stick sequins on each side of the row of windows.

Make each of the eight little flowers from two circles of blue or gold foil, one 30mm (1¼in.) and the other 25mm (1in.) in diameter. Divide the larger circle into six by keeping the compass set to the drawing radius and stepping this around the perimeter six times. This will make the six petals. Cut out the shape and mark the veins with a knitting needle. Bend the petals upwards to form the flower shape, and snip the smaller circle to form the flower center. Sew the two parts together, finishing off with a pearl or gold bead with a smaller pearl or bead on top. Draw the petals tightly together and knot the thread. Sew or glue the flowers to the paper cone, arranging them attractively. If you are short of time, the candle-holder angel can be decorated

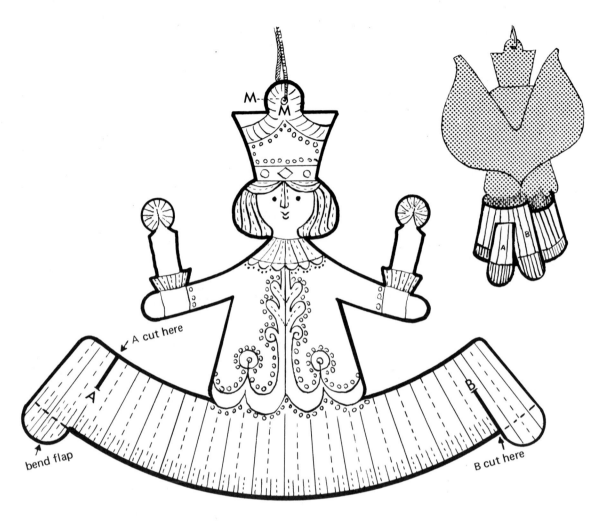

A cut here

bend flap

A

B

B cut here

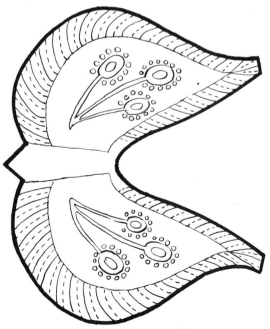

——————— cut round outline

- - - - - - mark from the front

——————— mark from the back

Trace the two nearest diagrams and follow the making-up diagram on the right and instructions opposite to obtain the silver and gold angel on page 61.

with foil stars and circles, or even painted.

Put on the head as already described, and stick on blue foil hair. Glue together the finished paper cone dress, and glue it to the neck cork.

The collar is made from a circle of gold foil 60mm (2⅜in.) in diameter, shaped as shown and decoratively stamped.

Make two more large flowers for the head, one in gold foil, the other in blue. Stick them firmly to the head, and bend the petals upward. They are not only decorative, but will catch drips from the candle which is placed on the screw.

The Advent candle angel on page 60 is made in the same way as just described, using the diagram alongside the photograph.

The silver foil is first painted with matt magenta paint and decorated by scraping while the paint is still wet. Foliage and dried flowers are pinned to the head and the hair is made from plaited black wool. The pictures in the Advent windows are painted on tracing paper to make them transparent, and each displays a different Christmas motif: candle, bell, ox, star, wise man, Mary and Joseph, and so on.

The wings are glued or sewn in place after embossing with a knitting needle.

The windows show best if the angel is placed over a low-power electric light; on no account should she be placed over a candle.

To make the angel (page 61, right), copy the two diagrams opposite on tracing paper. Stick the tracing paper on a piece of thick silver metal foil and trace over all the lines again so that they are lightly imprinted on the foil. The semicircle forming the base is best drawn with a pair of compasses: place the point at M with radii of 105mm (4⅛in.) and 80mm (3⅛in.). Cut around the outline of the figure and wings and imprint the design according to the key: dotted lines from the front, thin lines from the back.

Lay the foil on a soft surface, such as a pile of newspapers, and work over the lines with a blunt point such as a knitting needle or dry ballpoint pen. When inscribed from the back the lines appear embossed; inscribed from the front they appear engraved. The folds on the skirt are best made by laying a ruler through point M and working from there throughout.

Paint the figure and wings in bright colors. Bend the skirt around, slot together the cuts at A and B, bend the flaps to the inside, and press down as shown in the diagram (opposite, right).

The wings are glued to the back with clear adhesive. When the glue is dry, bend the wings backward and the arms forward. Pierce at point M and insert a thread for hanging.

Nativity scenes

Cloth sculpture is a craft which lends itself particularly well to a Nativity scene. It is inexpensive and easy to master and, under adult supervision, even the younger members of the family can become quite skilled at it.

The basic technique consists of dipping cloth into paste and draping it on a simple base to form a figure. When dry, the 'sculpture' is very strong and durable and can be painted or sprayed. Most of the materials can be found around the home. The main requirements are discarded cloth, cardboard cereal boxes, tissue paper, newspaper and cold water or cellulose (wallpaper) paste, which is available from decorating shops, and wire. Medium-gauge aluminium wire is best but any type can be used so long as it bends easily and stays in position. Other oddments needed are wool for hair, lace edgings, braids, beads, buttons and paints.

Make up the cold water paste according to the directions provided. It must be of the consistency of thick cream.

Making a cone-shaped figure

This is the basic shape for all figures and can be adapted for sitting and kneeling figures.

A large cereal box rolled into a cone shape (see fig. 1) will make a figure about 325mm (13in.) high. Trim the edges at the wider end of the cone to make it stand steadily. Make two holes near the narrow end of the cone. Cut a piece of wire 600mm (24in.) long. Insert the wire into the cone, bend it in half and twist it at the bent end to form the neck of the figure, and push the two ends of the wire through the holes to make the arms. Fold back two loops of wire for the hands (see fig. 2).

Make a head with roughly crumpled newspaper or tissue paper. Dip lightly into the paste and add layers of newspaper, gently molding the head into a large egg shape. As a rough guide to size, remember that the head is approximately one sixth of the size of the body. Do not make the head too large. If necessary you can build it up a bit more when it is dry, but it is very difficult to reduce the size.

Opposite: You can make all the figures and animals in this scene from one basic shape. Use fabric strips in various ways to give character and poise to each model. Spray them with gold paint for a striking appearance.

Take a pair of scissors and make a deep hole in the base of the head at the narrow end. Put this on top of the wire protruding from the cone. Add a few layers of pasted tissue paper to secure the head to the top part of the cone and the shoulder area, squeezing well into the neck and molding with the hands.

The body is now ready for draping with oblong and square shapes of cloth.

Draping

The figure of Mary in the Nativity scene has a finished height of 400mm (16in.), as do all the other standing models.

For the drapery you need a few 150 × 25mm (6 × 1in.) strips of fabric, one length about 600 × 250mm (24 × 10in.), one length about 750 × 350mm (30 × 14in.), two 175mm (7in.) squares, a small oval shape to cover the face and strands of wool for the hair.

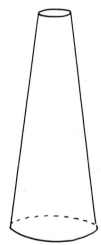

Fig. 1

Fig. 2

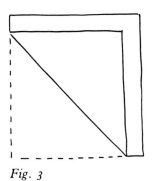

Fig. 3

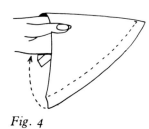

Fig. 4

Fig. 5

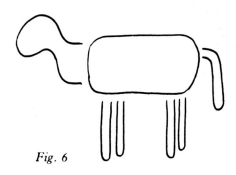

Fig. 6

Always work on newspaper, otherwise it will be impossible to remove the finished model successfully.

Take the thin strips of cloth and dip them into the paste. Squeeze out the surplus, smooth out the material and wind the strips around the hands and lower parts of the arms. The whole of the wire arms and shoulders can be covered if you like. Mold the hands into shape.

Take the largest piece of cloth and cut two small holes in the longer side, 40mm (1½in.) down and 225mm (9in.) in from the ends of the cloth. Submerge this piece in paste, then remove and squeeze out the surplus paste. Hold the cloth up in one hand and run the other along the cloth to remove the surplus paste, straightening out the cloth while doing so. Fold down the hem on the long side of the cloth opposite the holes, to hide the raw edges.

Dressing

Feed the arms through the holes made in the cloth. Gather up the fullness into tiny pleats around the neck. Join the material at the center back by overlapping it. The drapery can be arranged into as many neat folds as possible. For extra strength this main drapery can be secured at the neck by binding it with a thin strip of cloth.

To make the sleeves, take the 175mm (7in.) squares, dip in paste, squeeze and partly fold over one corner to form a triangle (see fig. 3). Fold over the hand as in fig. 4. Put this shape over the arm, pointed end to the top of the arm, and press to shape. Take the medium-sized piece of cloth. Dip in paste as above, and fold under a small hem all the way around to hide raw edges. Drape this cloth over head and shoulders. Paste the small oval shape and cover the face with this.

Drying and painting

Leave to dry in a warm place. Models can be dried out quickly on a baking sheet in a very low oven with the door left ajar to let the steam escape. Decorate when dry. Gold and copper spray looks effective, or the figures can be painted with most kinds of paint.

Sitting or kneeling figures can be made by using smaller cones (215mm, 8½in.) (see fig. 5) with wire legs bent to shape. Make holes for the legs in the lower front edge of the cone, passing the wire through one hole and out of the other.

These sheep are easy to make. Mold the bodies from tissue paper dipped in paste. Make the basic leg, tail and head shapes with wire (see fig. 6). The body becomes very hard when completely dry; then you can insert wire shapes in it. Fill out the wire parts with pasted tissue paper, molding them to the body to keep them in place. To give the sheep fleece, paste cotton wool over the main areas.

Making animals

Make a wire outline of the animal to be modeled. Secure the ends with adhesive tape. Make oval-shaped wire frames to fit over and around the body and head of the animal; this will give it fullness and a rounded appearance. Bend lengths of wire into shape for the legs and ears, and attach them with tape to the framework. Pad the wire shape with crumpled newspaper pushed inside it and bind the legs with strips of pasted cloth. Cover the body with 75mm (3in.) square patches of pasted cloth. Squeeze and mold the animal into shape.

Christmas cribs

To make these realistic-looking Christmas cribs, you will need certain tools and materials. The tools are: a fretsaw, a drill with a 3mm (⅛in.) bit, a file, sandpaper, wire-cutting pliers, flat pliers, scissors and implements from a manicure set (page 70, bottom left) for modeling the clay.

To make the kneeling shepherd or seated Mother, reduce a 330mm (13in.) cone by cutting off the wide base area, leaving a small cone measuring 240mm (9½in.) Drape the model in the usual way, placing the full-length main drape of the kneeling figure under the bottom of the cone and out at the back of the model. Cut lengths of folder or rolled card to make the shepherd's lower legs and put them under the drape at the back. Make feet by molding pasted tissue paper and press them into position on the ends of the cardboard legs, so that they are just visible among the folds of cloth.

An orange stick will also be useful for this. Materials include balsa wood 15mm (⅝in.) thick, brass or copper wire (heavy, medium and light, one spool each), aluminium wire 3mm (⅛in.) thick, modeling clay which will fire in an oven, cardboard in various thicknesses, sewing thread, white tissue paper, glue, scraps of fabric, sequins and beads. The male figures are about 175mm (7in.) high, the women and children being proportionately smaller.

Making the figures

Cut the trunk in balsa wood with the saw to the shape illustrated on page 70, rounding off the edges with a file and sandpaper. Drill holes for the head, arms and legs. The thick wire will later be inserted into these holes.

Make this stable and the one on page 72 from bark, roots, moss and twigs. Cut and shape all these natural materials to make an appropriate Nativity setting. Use clay for the walls and roofs of caves or stables; apply it to rough-surfaced wooden boards for a really strong effect. Make sure that the stable remains in the background and does not dominate the Nativity scene.

To model heads, take a piece of aluminium wire long enough to afford a good grasp and wrap around it a strip of thin cardboard about 40mm (1½in.) wide—three turns are sufficient. To keep the roll from unwinding, wrap thread around the cardboard and coat it with glue. The top of the roll must be well sealed to prevent the wire poking through the head later on.

Cut tissue paper into 25mm (1in.) wide strips and wrap these strips around the cardboard roll to make the shape of the head and neck. Glue each layer of tissue paper to make it stronger. (See pictures on page 71.)

Prepare modeling clay to the consistency of thick paste, add a little glue and shape the head in detail with the aid of the manicure tools. Be careful to make the neck long enough, as it is easier to shorten it than it is to lengthen it. Use the same method of construction for the hands. The wire should be about 25mm (1in.) long, and two turns of cardboard will suffice. Then shape a piece of brass wire for the hands. (See illustra-

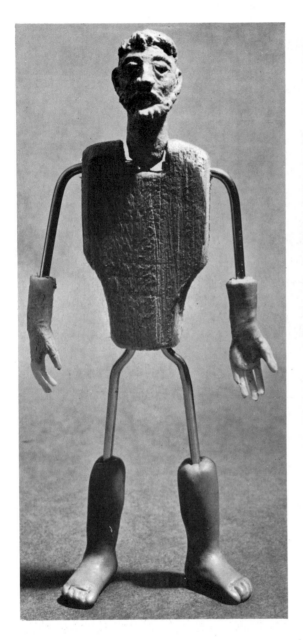

Make a figure with a skeleton like this.

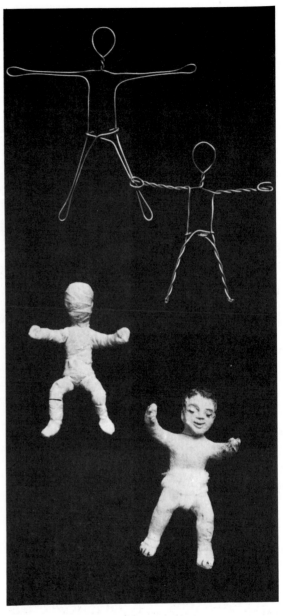

The four stages in making the Holy Child.

Manicure implements are useful for modeling fine details.

tion page 71.) Insert arms and head into the body when dry. Feet and legs are shaped directly on the bare wire with heavier modeling clay.

To make the Child

This little figure is not jointed like the others. For this figure, you need a wire armature, as shown above, which is covered in tissue paper and glue, built up until it is the right shape. To

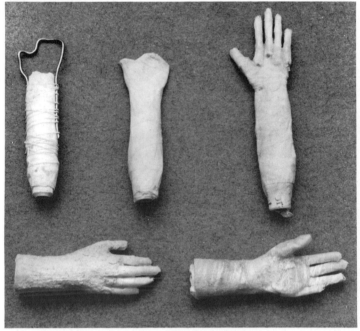

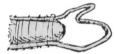

Above: *Details of the construction of arms, hands and heads.*

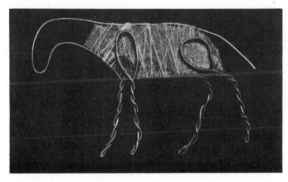

make the wrapping easier, put a ball of paper into the head and body loops. When the forms have all been filled out, wrap the figure around, give it a coat of glue, and bend it into position.

Animals

These are an essential part of a Nativity scene. Cut a piece of stiff cardboard into the shape shown above and wrap around it a piece of wire, with a loop for the head and an extension for the tail. Tie the wire to the cardboard with thread. Bend pieces of wire to make the legs.

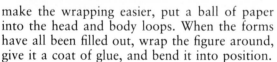

Three stages in making an animal. Adapt this figure to make a sheep, horse or donkey.

A variation of the Nativity scene on page 69 including the three Wise Men. Their rich array contrasts strongly with the plain, simple clothes of Mary and Joseph and the stable.

Wrap with tissue paper, glue them to the body, and secure the joints with more thread. Fill the rest of the body in with tissue paper and glue. Coat the whole thing with glue. When dry, finish off with modeling clay. Dogs, sheep, donkeys and oxen can all be made in the same way.

Painting

Coat the surfaces to be colored with glue so that the paint will take well. Either watercolor or tempera color can be used successfully. After painting, spray with clear varnish.

Dressing

Sew together the sleeves of a dress or tunic, leaving a short length unsewn at the upper end, as this part will now be glued directly to the shoulders. Sew on sleeves last.

The stable, pictured in both illustrations, is made from some boards of balsa wood and a roof of bark and straw. A few twigs make wintery-looking trees.

Metal foil Nativity scene

To make these symbolic, almost abstract figures of the Holy Family, you need double-sided metal foil. This can be bought from almost any crafts shop. The only tools needed are pencil and ruler, compasses and scissors, glue and a craft knife. So that the scene will not be too gaudy, limit the colors to about four (red, blue, silver and gold are used in the illustration opposite). The pat-

A Nativity scene made entirely from metal foil, together with patterns for the figures (all shown half-size).

terns shown here are one half actual size and, except for the Child, show only half of each figure.

Cut out the figures to the patterns overleaf, making them as large as you wish, and form the bodies of the Virgin and Joseph into cones, gluing the overlapping flaps at the back and bending the arms to the front of each of the bodies.

The figure of the Virgin is cut from blue foil and the hands and face are of gold foil glued to the basic figure. Attach the red shawl to the face of the Virgin, joining it with a narrow band of the same color underneath the chin.

Joseph is formed of a silver foil cone. Glue on an apron and arms in blue, a silver headdress with a blue circlet (as in the diagram) and a thick gold foil beard made by fringing a small piece of foil and curling it around a pencil.

In making the Child the foil is cut out and shaped so that the small inner circle forms the head, the narrow circle forms the halo and the

semicircle forms the arms. Cut the arms only as far as the two arrows indicated on the diagram and cut away the shaded area completely to reveal the head beneath the halo. Bend the two arms forward.

The crib is a 100mm (4in.) square of blue foil with semicircles glued on the head and the foot. Finish with a red background and a large star.

Nativity figures

Christmas scenes do not have to be elaborate. These simple figures (*opposite*), so primitive in style that they resemble the timeless crib scenes of Mexico and South America, are very easy to make.

Our figures were made with the basic tools to be found about the house, such as a kitchen knife and a few matches, and they were colored with bright poster paints. The modeling is so straightforward that any child could attempt it.

They can be made in any of the new self-hardening modeling clays that are obtainable from most crafts shops. When dry, our figures were painted and then varnished with a special varnish

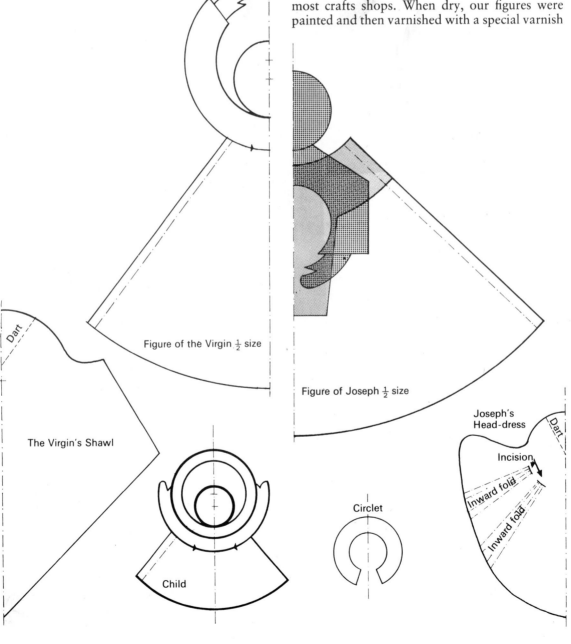

Dart

Figure of the Virgin ½ size

The Virgin's Shawl

Figure of Joseph ½ size

Joseph's Head-dress

Dart

Incision

Inward fold

Inward fold

Child

Circlet

This scene is made from self-hardening clay which is painted, then covered in a special varnish.

that is made to go with the clay. You could use an ordinary spray-on varnish to protect the paint and make the figures less liable to be damaged. Or you could paint them with oil-based enamel paints, in which case they would not need to be varnished.

There is not even any need to go to a crafts shop and spend money, as there is another modeling material which can be used for this type of figure and it is one that is easily made at home.

This is flour and water dough (baker's clay), baked in the oven.

To make enough dough for, say, half a dozen small figures, you would need three large cups of plain flour, three cups of salt, and one cup of cold water. Coloring can be included in the dough or added later. If it is to be included, use food coloring. Mix up the ingredients in a bowl and knead the dough well for several minutes.

Make a ball of dough for the head and a roll of dough long enough for the body. Join the head and body with water, then model the hands, features and details. Bake the figures flat on a baking tin in a low oven until they are quite

hard. Sandpaper smooth any rough areas, then paint and finally varnish the figures.

Whatever modeling material you use, make the details, such as the decorations of the robes, the headdresses, faces and so on, very simple in shape. Circles and dots can be made by poking the head of a match into the clay or dough while it is still damp. Triangular or diamond shapes can be cut into the clay with a knife and the hands can also be modeled with a sharp-pointed kitchen knife. Keep the features and accessories, simple too, as such as stars, trees and animals, simple too, as they are in our illustration. Note how the leaves of the trees are boldly modeled, some with veins incised with a knife, others left plain. A lot of fussy detail would detract from the charm of these touchingly simple figures.

When the self-hardening clay is dry, paint the figures carefully. Patience at this stage will be rewarded. Flour-and-water dough is an excellent substitute for clay, but you must bake it in an oven before painting.

Pine-cone figures

Pine-cones are readily available and cost nothing and they too can form the basis of Nativity figures, like those illustrated on page 78. This type of scene is purely symbolic, so no attempt should be made to achieve a realistic effect.

You need long pine-cones, not the short fat ones. Start by sawing the points off the cones so that they can be glued on to cardboard or wooden disks to enable them to stand steadily. The wooden or polystyrene balls forming the heads are glued on with clear glue, thus giving the figures a neck. Prepare all the figures the same way. Heads and bodies can be held together with rubber bands while the glue dries. The figures are then identified by their clothing and accessories.

Mary wears a blue cloak of soft fabric, which goes over her head, and her hair can be made from flax, hemp, wool or silk.

Joseph has woollen hair and he is wearing a slouch hat and a dark cloak made of a scrap of fabric. Make the hat from a circle of blue felt, glued to a cork which has been cut short and painted blue to match.

You can make a very simple, symbolic Nativity scene with pine-cones for figures, sandpaper-covered wood for the floor, lichen for the bushes, and a large straw star.

The three kings should be dressed as colorfully as possible, with cloaks of felt in brilliant colors and crowns made of gold braid. Hair can be of silk, wool or cotton wool (absorbent cotton), suitably colored.

The baby Jesus is made from a small pine-cone with a pink-painted polystyrene ball for a head. He has very fine hair, the sort that is sold for making dolls' hair.

To make all the cloaks, cut large or small semicircles of felt, lay them around the figure and either glue them in place at the back of the neck or tack them together at the front with needle and thread.

The stable floor is made from a piece of wood covered with sandpaper, which is glued on. Two lengths of split willow arch over the top. They are crossed in the center and nailed to the short edges of the board. An ornamental straw star is stuck to the center of the arch, over the whole scene. The curly 'bushes' on the stable floor are made from the type of lichen which is sold in railway modeler's shops to represent trees, but you could also use scraps of green-painted plastic foam, green-painted sponge or dried moss.

Right: *Make all the figures in the scene from the basic patterns shown above. Bend and shape them into the desired poses when they are ready.*

Straw figures

Straw must be well softened for making Nativity figures; it should be soaked for an hour in warm water. The basic method of making the figures is the same for all of them. You need natural straws, clear glue, a sharp knife, strong thread and raffia. Variations in color (from pale biscuit to dark brown) can be achieved by ironing with a hot iron, or straw can be bought ready-dyed.

Bind eight straws tightly together about 12mm (½in.) from one end with raffia (diagram a, overleaf). Form the head by turning the bundle the other way up and bending all the straws over and down; tie around firmly at the neck (diagram

b). To make the arms, either plait or twist several straws together like a cord, or make a 'witches' staircase'. To do this, lay two straws at right angles to each other, one over the other, then keep bending the lower one over the upper (diagram c). The arms should be pushed through the straws immediately under the head and bound in place tightly (diagram d). For the skirt, lay 12 straws around the figure so that the long ends stick upward; tie tightly around and bend the long ends down (diagram e). Cut the straws to the required length.

Now for the refinements. First dress the upper

part of the figure. Mary has a cloak made from straws, cut short in front and left long behind, which hide the join of the skirt. Joseph has a mantle, made from three straws left equally long back and front. Joseph's lantern is made from short lengths of straw glued together, his staff is a long stout straw glued to the hand. Mary, Joseph and the baby Jesus all have haloes made from very narrow strips of straw, carefully glued in place.

A kneeling figure such as Mary can be difficult to achieve at first. A useful tip is to bind the damp straw into the required position. When it is dry, remove the binding and the figure will remain in shape.

The baby Jesus is made in much the same way as the other figures. The straws forming the body are tightly bound around with more straws to form swaddling bands and hide the cut ends at the bottom. Provided the straw is damp enough, the binding is not too difficult to do.

The three kings are especially beautiful, as colored straw is used for them. The creation of the crowns, garments and gifts is a rewarding exercise in plaiting and binding. The standing king is made from dark rye straw.

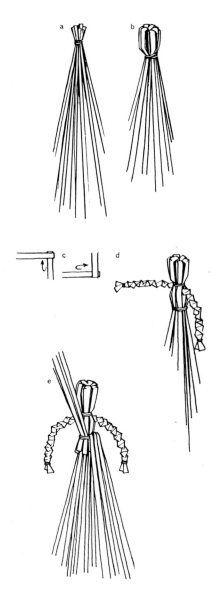

Above: *Stages in making a straw figure.*

Christmas cards

Making your own cards will not only save you money, but will also provide you with a means of sending your Christmas message in a completely personal way.

Materials

For your base card it is better to buy a selection of colored papers and cardboard, rather than to buy a white card and try to color it yourself. For lino-prints and stencils, you may find it easier to produce your design on an absorbent paper or tissue before mounting it on a base card.

Even the simplest design can be made more striking by attractive colored mounts, so choose the colors of your base cards carefully and experiment by laying one color on top of another for pleasing results.

Rubber cement is recommended for most gluing. It will not soak through your paper, can be cleaned off easily if it gets on to the picture surface, and also allows pictures to be repositioned if necessary.

Sharp scissors are essential. A craft knife or scalpel is recommended for fine cutting out, and is used in conjunction with a metal-edged ruler for trimming your cards to size.

Reusing old cards

Using a ruler and set-square, draw an outline around the illustration to be used. Cut out the illustration using a craft-knife against the edge of a metal ruler. Select a matching paper and glue the illustration to it, leaving a border of about 6mm (¼in.) all the way around. Trim the paper as necessary.

Fold a piece of colored cardboard and trim it to the required size for your finished card. Place your mounted illustration on the base card and move it around until you are satisfied with its position. Use a ruler and set-square to check that it is placed squarely on the base card, then make small pencil marks at each corner. Apply glue to the back of the illustration and attach it to the

Page 81: An attractive selection of cards made with the techniques described in this chapter. They are (from left to right) top row: stencil, pressed flowers, stencil, old card re-used; center row: gummed paper, old card, gummed paper; bottom row: old card, a simple traced and painted design, pressed flowers, and another re-used old card.

base card using the four pencil marks as a guide. Place the completed card under a pile of books until the glue is quite set.

Collage

Collage consists of cutting out and pasting down paper and other materials to make a picture or design. Our collage cards have all been created from magazine and book illustrations, and you will see that it is possible to produce either semi-realistic or surrealist compositions. Make a collection of newspaper and magazine photographs, old greetings cards, calendars, postcards, and so on, and you are ready to begin.

All elements for the collage must be cut out with great care, so use small, sharp scissors, and a craft knife for fine work. When you have selected your cut-outs, place them on a base card or photograph, and move them around until you create a pleasing effect. Cover the backs of the cut-outs with a thin layer of rubber cement and place them on the card. Remove any surplus rubber cement with your fingertip or a small piece of dried rubber cement, taking care not to damage the edges of your cut-outs.

Gummed paper cut-outs

These are made from gummed paper squares which are obtainable in packs of assorted colors. You can also buy packs of ready-cut gummed paper shapes which you can combine with your own cut-outs, or use on their own if you prefer.

Trace your own design, or copy one of ours on tracing paper. Place a piece of carbon paper face down on a piece of gummed paper with your tracing on top. Trace over the design again with a hard pencil until the complete design has been transferred to the gummed paper. Cut around the outlines on the paper, cutting three or four sheets together if you need more than one copy of the same design. Wet the gummed surface of the cut-out with a damp sponge, and press it firmly in position on a base card of a contrasting color. Leave the completed card under a pile of books until the gum has dried.

Small details which are too fine to cut out can be added later with a fiber-tip pen or poster colors.

Stencils

Stencils provide a useful method of duplicating the same design. The design shapes are cut out

These colorful cards show the results obtained by carefully matching base cards with pictures from old cards, books and magazines. Add embellishments with fiber-tip pens or gummed-paper borders.

from waterproof waxed cardboard or parchment, and then color is applied through the holes to leave a clearly defined design on the paper or cardboard beneath.

You can buy ready-made stencils if you do not have time to cut out your own, or you can buy a book of stencil designs, which can be cut out directly from the book. (The pages need to be treated with boiled linseed oil to make them waterproof.)

Choose a simple, bold design when making your own stencils. Large areas should be broken up with links, which, as well as serving to hold the stencil plate together, are one of the main characteristics of stencil work.

Make a tracing of your selected design and transfer it to the stencil cardboard by using carbon paper. Use black paint or fiber-tip pens to color the parts of the design which are to be cut out. Cut out the shapes very carefully, exerting an even pressure for the entire length of a line or curve.

Eight collage cards made from magazine and book illustrations.

Tape the cut stencil to the paper or cardboard which you intend to print, making sure that it is securely fixed, as any movement will cause the design to smear.

Mix your chosen colors to a thick consistency. Water-based acrylic paints are ideal as they are fast-drying and of the right consistency for stencil work. Select a stencil brush and dip the flat bottom of the bristles into the paint, taking care not to overload the brush. Hold the brush like a

pencil and make rapid up and down movements to stipple the color through the cut-out openings in the stencil until the design is transferred to the paper beneath.

Wait until the stencil is completely dry before removing the stencil plate. If you want to print your design in more than one color, unwanted areas should be obscured by masking tape. When the first color has dried completely, cover those parts of the stencil with tape. Remove the tape

*Four cards made from gummed paper cut-outs. The
reindeer's eye was painted black with a fiber-tip pen.*

from the previously covered areas and apply the
second color.

As an alternative to brush stippling you may
prefer to work with an inexpensive spray diffuser. These can be obtained quite cheaply from
artist's suppliers and are operated by inserting
one end of the diffuser into the paint or ink to
be sprayed and the other end into the mouth.
Blowing through the mouthpiece causes the paint
to be drawn up the tube and diffused from a

small hole at the center. Experiment with paint
of various consistencies until you find the right
one. And use plenty of old newspapers to protect
surrounding areas from the spray!

Lino-prints

Draw a bold design directly on to the lino with
a soft pencil, or trace it first, and use carbon

Nine cards made with stencils. Four of the cards were produced in two colors by obscuring part of the design with masking tape. After coloring the exposed areas, let them dry, cover them with masking tape, and color the previously covered areas. The design on the card in the middle of the bottom row was made by using a diffuser to spray color through a household doily. You can also use stencil designs to cover wrapping papers, but take care that each print is dry before repeating.

paper to transfer your design. Remember that the shapes you cut from the lino will appear as white on the final print, and that all prints will appear as a mirror-image of your cut design. Use black water-based paint to color those parts of the design which are to be retained for printing, to avoid mistakes when cutting.

Cut around the edges of the design, using a craft knife or scalpel, to a depth of about 6mm (¼in.). Use a gouging lino-cutting tool to remove large areas of lino, and a fine tool for the rest, always directing the cutting tool away from yourself to avoid accidents.

Six cards made from the same lino-cut with various colors and papers.
Tissue paper is an ideal printing surface. The range of attractive colors will add variety to your cards even when you use the same design. Mount prints on the fronts of base cards with rubber cement, or alternatively, glue them behind a cut-out frame to give a stained-glass window effect.

Roll a small quantity of water-based printing ink on a sheet of glass until the roller makes a 'smacking' sound. Roll an even layer of ink over the lino surface and place a piece of absorbent tissue on top. Rub over the back of the paper with the back of a spoon or a clean roller, exerting as much pressure as possible in order to ensure a well-defined print.

Finally, peel off the paper with one hand while holding the lino steady with the other.

CHRISTMAS CRAFTS

An angel stencil design for you to trace and cut out in stencil paper. There is a finished card using this design in the center of the middle row in the photograph on page 86. Cut the design very carefully, using a sharp craft knife or scalpel. After printing, gently wipe stencil plates with a damp cloth to remove traces of paint, dry them flat, and store carefully for future use.

Pressed flowers

To press simple flowers and leaves, fold a sheet of blotting paper in half and arrange dry, freshly picked flowers neatly and well spaced on one side, carefully flattening each specimen as you work. Fold over the other half of the blotting sheet, and place the package between wads of newspaper folded to the same size. Cover with an even distribution of heavy books or weights, and after about ten days replace the soiled newspapers and reposition the weights, without disturbing the flowers. Leave the pressings undisturbed in a warm, dry atmosphere for about a month.

Make your cards in a draft-free room out of direct sunlight. Remove your pressings from the blotting paper with tweezers, and move them around on your cards with a small paint brush, so as to avoid damaging the delicate structures.

Various pressed flowers. The background colors have been chosen not to detract from the delicate natural colors. Combining a flower with foliage from another plant can be effective. It is not important to use foliage from the same plant as the flower.

If you think your cards are worth framing, protect them with clear cellophane instead of self-adhesive film, but always put them between two pieces of stiff cardboard before posting them to friends.

Don't lay petals over stalks, as they may bruise. When you have decided on your design, apply minute quantities of a gentle, quick-drying, non-staining adhesive to the back of the flowers using a toothpick, and attach the flowers to the card.

Remove any loose fragments of petals with the paint brush, and protect your pressings with a clear self-adhesive film.

Paper chains

Making your own paper chains is an absorbing way to occupy the long winter evenings leading up to Christmas and will provide you with original and colorful decorations at a fraction of the cost of ready-made varieties.

Materials

You will need a selection of colored tissue paper, a few sheets of cartridge or colored drawing papers, a few sheets of thin card (pasteboard), a pair of scissors, a needle and thread (or a stapler), and some glue. The best glues for the purpose are those sold in lipstick-type tubes, or those specially recommended for tissue paper. If you are in doubt, experiment with some glue on scraps of tissue paper before applying it to your paper chains.

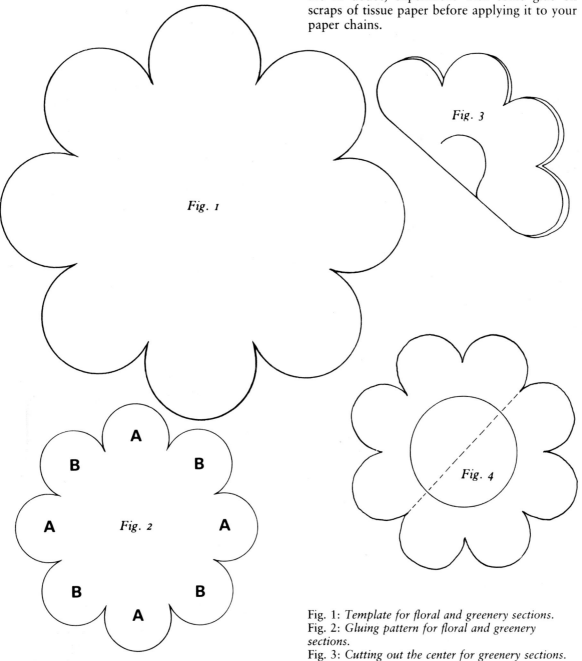

Opposite: A floral garland with greenery. Instructions for making this are on page 92.

Fig. 1: *Template for floral and greenery sections.*
Fig. 2: *Gluing pattern for floral and greenery sections.*
Fig. 3: *Cutting out the center for greenery sections.*
Fig. 4: *Cutting tabs from thin card (pasteboard) for fastening at either end of the completed chain.*

A floral garland with greenery

Floral sections

A template of thin card (pasteboard) will save a lot of time and enable you to cut all your tissue paper shapes to the same size, so begin by tracing the outline shown in fig. 1 on the previous page. Using carbon paper under your tracing, transfer the outline to a piece of thin card (pasteboard) and cut out the shape.

Using the template as a guide, cut out a number of pieces of tissue in your chosen color. Take the first piece of tissue and apply a small dab of glue at each of the points marked A in fig. 2. Take a second tissue cut-out, place it accurately on top of the first, and apply a small dab of glue at the points marked B. Place a third tissue shape on top, and glue it at the points marked A. Continue gluing alternate sheets in this way until you have a floral garland of the required length.

Remember that the more carefully you apply the glue and the more accurately you position the tissue cut-outs, the better the final result will be.

Greenery sections

Using the template in fig. 1, cut shapes from green tissue paper. Fold the tissue shapes in half, and cut a semicircle from the center so as to form a complete circle when the tissues are opened out (fig. 3).

Apply small dabs of glue on alternate lobes, as shown in fig. 2, to join the sheets together. These shapes are more fragile than those used for the floral sections, so to avoid the risk of tearing, you will need to position your thumb and forefinger on either side of the point being glued.

Combine your completed floral and greenery sections in any way that you wish, and cut two circles from thin card (pasteboard) for use at the beginning and end of your garland. These should be trimmed slightly smaller than the tissue paper shape. Fold the circles in half, and cut tabs in the centers for use when fastening to the wall or ceiling (fig. 4).

Simple paper chains

This is a very quick way of producing long lengths of decoration, and is simple enough for a young child to enjoy.

Prepare a number of tissue sheets approximately 160 × 45mm (6¼ × 1¾in.) and glue them according to the gluing pattern shown in fig. 5, the first sheet at A, the second at B, the third at A, and so on.

You can leave the edges of your cut-out shapes plain, or for a more interesting effect, use a template and scallop the edges.

Paper chains with hanging blossom

Cut a number of tissue paper shapes from the scallop pattern shown in fig. 5. You can use more

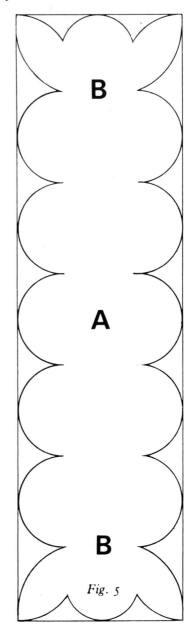

Fig. 5

Fig. 5: *Template and gluing pattern for a simple paper chain.*

A simple multi-colored paper chain and a simple paper chain with hanging blossom.

than one color for the chain—we have used green and blue; and a third color for the blossom, which we have made in pink.

Making the blossom sections

Use five tissue paper shapes for each section. Follow the gluing pattern shown in fig. 6, gluing the first sheet at *A*, the second at *B*, the third at *A*, and so on. When you reach the fifth sheet,

glue it, and fold all the sheets in half as shown in fig. 7. (Figs. 6 and 7 overleaf.)

Fixing the chain and blossom together

The use of two colors for the chain will help you keep count when you are placing the blossoms. We fixed our blossom between two blue tissues with two green tissues on either side.

Glue the first sheet at *A* and the second sheet at *B*. Glue the third sheet at *A*, but, to make the blossom spread out, also glue it at *C* (fig. 8).

Position the blossom section and glue it at *A*

and C (fig. 9). Place the fourth chain tissue and glue it at B, and so on.

Ornaments for the tree

For each of these attractive Christmas tree decorations you will need a thin piece of card (pasteboard) and 30 sheets of tissue paper cut in circles of 75mm (3in.) diameter (fig. 10).

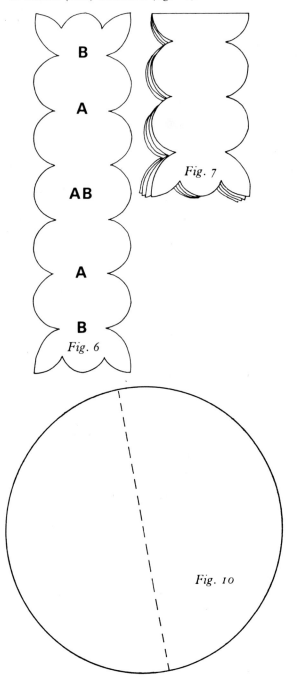

Fig. 6

Fig. 7

Fig. 10

Fastening the tissue paper sheets

Fold the tissue paper sheets and the card (pasteboard) exactly in half to find the center line. The tissue and card (pasteboard) should be fastened together either by sewing or by using the stapler. A simple 'three-hole' book-binding stitch is used for sewing (fig. 11). Leave 25mm (1in.) or so of thread hanging from the center, and after you have pulled the needle through the third hole, pass it under the first stitch and tie the two ends of thread together (fig. 12).

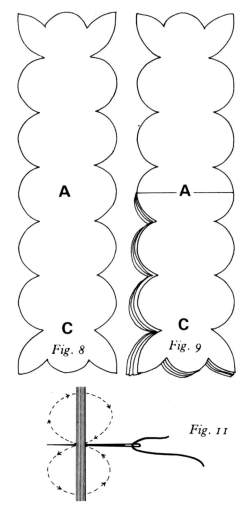

Fig. 8

Fig. 9

Fig. 11

Fig. 6: *Gluing pattern for the blossom sections.*
Fig. 7: *The blossom section is folded in half after gluing.*
Fig. 8: *Glue the third sheet at A, but glue at C to make the blossom spread out.*
Fig. 9: *The blossom section glued to a chain tissue.*
Fig. 10: *Template for round ornaments for the tree.*
Fig. 11: *A simple three-hole bookbinding stitch for fastening tissue cut-outs to a piece of card (pasteboard).*

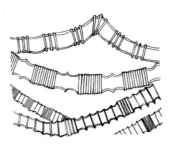

Colorful tree ornaments in blending colors. These are all made in the same color combinations, but you can use any colors.

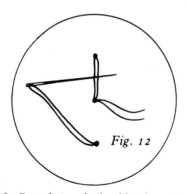

Fig. 12: *Completing the bookbinding stitch.*

Gluing the leaves

With the tissue paper side lying face downward, fold the piece of card (pasteboard) back on itself as it will be when the ball is fully opened out. Pick up the first tissue paper sheet and glue it firmly to the card (pasteboard). The second sheet of tissue should be glued to the first at the points marked *A* in fig. 13, the third at points marked *B*, the fourth at points marked *A*, and so on, until you reach the final sheet. (See overleaf.)

Turn the 'book' over and glue the other halves of the tissue paper circles in the same way. This time, when you reach the final sheet, glue it at points marked *A* and *B*, and fold the card to meet it so that the two are joined together (fig. 14 overleaf).

Note. When applying glue to these open-out shapes, try to keep it inside the edge of the paper, otherwise you will find that the shapes are difficult to open. Always give the glue plenty of

time to set before attempting to open out the shape. Even so, you may still find that one or two points need to be re-glued.

Fasten a piece of thread at the back of the card for hanging, and use paper clips or staples to keep the shape open.

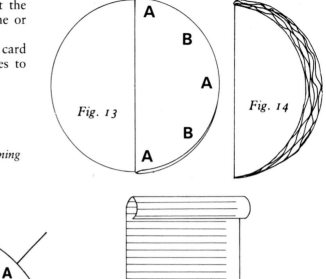

Fig. 13

Fig. 14

Fig. 13: *Gluing pattern for the tree ornaments.*
Fig. 14: *The completed ornament ready for opening out.*

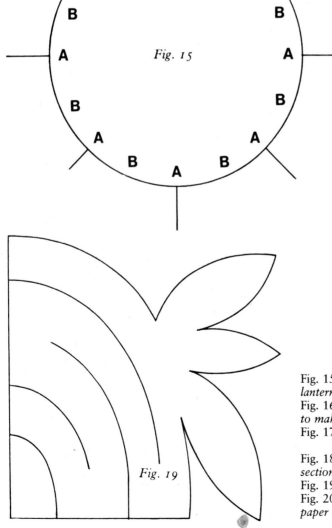

Fig. 15

Fig. 16

Fig. 19

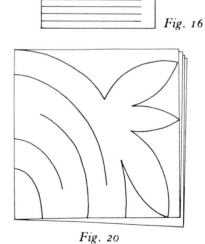

Fig. 20

Fig. 15: *Template and gluing pattern for hanging lanterns.*
Fig. 16: *After cutting, roll a rectangle of tissue paper to make tassels.*
Fig. 17: *Complete tassels with a circle of metal foil.*

Fig. 18: *Template and gluing pattern for flower sections.*
Fig. 19: *Template for the paper vine.*
Fig. 20: *The vine template placed on a piece of green paper folded in four.*

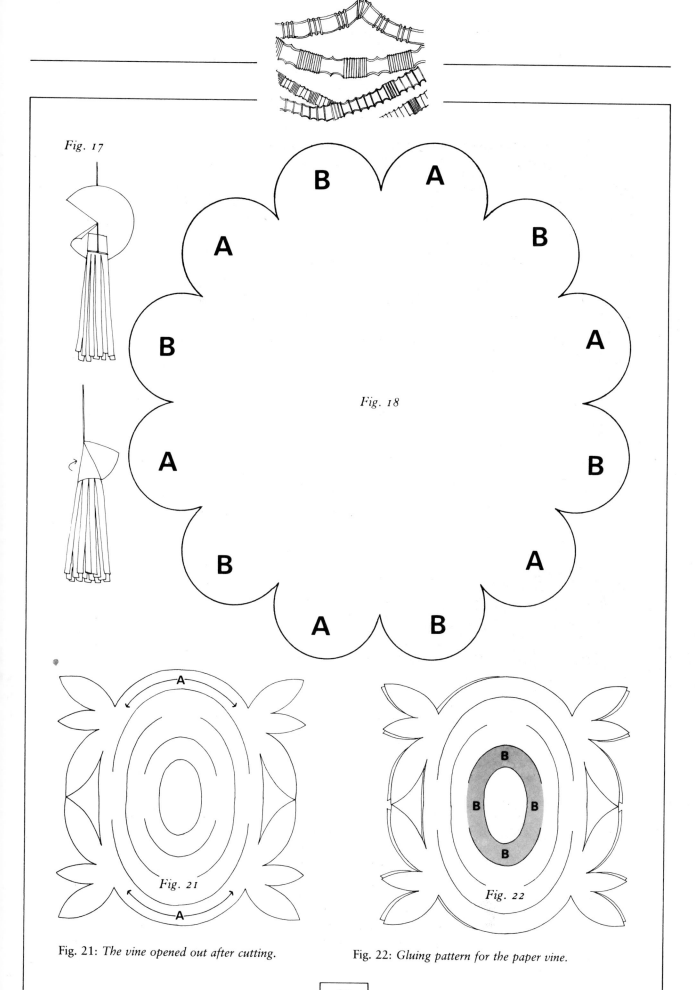

Fig. 17

Fig. 18

B   A

A   B

B   A

A   B

B   A

A   B

Fig. 21

A

A

Fig. 22

B

B   B

B

Fig. 21: *The vine opened out after cutting.*

Fig. 22: *Gluing pattern for the paper vine.*

Hanging lanterns. One plain and two patterned lanterns made by alternating leaves of different-colored tissue paper.

Hanging lanterns

You will need about 30 tissue paper circles of approximately 70mm (2¾in.) diameter for each lantern.

Follow the gluing guide shown in fig. 15, gluing sheets alternately at points *A* and *B* to fasten them together. When all the sheets have been glued, trim the edges for a neat finish. Cut a circle from the center of the pile of glued shapes and fasten the bottom sheet of tissue to a circular card (pasteboard) base.

Cut tassels from a tissue rectangle (fig. 16), roll, and secure the uncut edge with thread. Decorate the top of the tassel with a circle of metal foil (fig. 17) and stitch it on the lantern.

Finally, glue a circle of card (pasteboard) with a cut-out center to the top of the lantern, and attach thread for hanging.

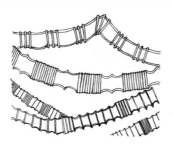

An attractive floral garland with a pull-out paper vine.

Floral garland with a pull-out paper vine

Making the flower sections

These floral sections have been made in exactly the same way as those in the floral garland described on page 91. The only difference is that here the tissue paper shapes have been cut to a larger size.

Make a template from the drawing shown in fig. 18 and use it as a guide to cut out a number of brightly colored tissue paper shapes which will form the flowers.

Take the first piece of tissue and apply a small dab of glue at each of the points marked *A* in fig. 18. Take the second piece of tissue, place it accurately on top of the first, and glue it at the points marked *B*. Place a third tissue on top, and glue it at points marked *A*. Continue gluing alternate sheets in this way until you have glued about 30 sheets, which will complete one flower section.

Making the paper vine

Trace the shape shown in fig. 19 and make a template in thin card (pasteboard). Place the template on a piece of green cartridge or drawing paper which has been folded in four (fig. 20). Cut around the edge of the template and also along the four inner lines shown in fig. 19. When the cut-out shape is opened it should look like that shown in fig. 21.

Prepare a number of these vines and glue them together in pairs at the points marked *A* in fig. 21.

Attach the flower sections between two pairs of vines, applying glue to the inner edges of the vines at point *B* as shown in fig. 22.

Gifts to make

Above: *Make these three clowns with pipe cleaners, paper balls, paper eggs, plastic caps from medicine and pill containers, mustard tube caps, wool, and wooden beads. The bases are three plastic lids with green felt stuck on top.*

Opposite: *Make these two warriors with eggs, decorated with felt scraps. Use medicine bottle corks, wooden skewers, rug wool, paper balls and mustard tube caps.*

It is often very difficult to decide what presents to buy for family and friends for birthdays and Christmas. Either you cannot find quite what you are looking for or the gift you do find is far too expensive to buy. So this chapter is full of unusual ideas for gifts to make which will each be personal and which will cost very much less than anything you could buy in a shop.

Pipe cleaner figures

You can buy pipe cleaners in all possible colors, either from tobacco shops or from handicrafts shops. The other materials needed are mostly those that are found about the house, such as the caps from toothpaste tubes, medicine bottle tops, small jar lids, plastic screw-tops from pill containers, the tops from felt- or fiber-tip pens, and anything else that comes to hand.

Also useful are florist's foam, cotton wool (absorbent cotton) and paper balls, colored wooden beads, blown or foam eggs, small scraps of felt, corks, lengths of wool, and fiber-tip pens.

For the parts that need gluing, use a good all-purpose clear glue.

Pipe cleaner figures can be cut with an old pair of scissors or a pair of pliers. To pierce paper balls in order to thread them, use a bradawl or a fine gimlet. A pair of tweezers is useful for holding pieces while gluing, and a craft knife is useful for shaping corks.

Begin by making the basic figures for the clowns. Use pipe cleaners, threaded through plastic caps from tubes and containers. The center clown has a body made from a large plastic lid, with holes drilled in it. The trousers are two small mustard tube caps and another mustard tube cap forms the high collar of the right-hand clown. The heads are made from 30mm (1¼in.) diameter paper balls, with long rug wool hair and features added with a fiber-tip pen. The legs are threaded with an assortment of wooden and paper balls, and paper eggs represent baggy trousers. The clowns stand on plastic lids.

The warriors on page 100 are based on eggs, decorated with felt scraps. Use blown real eggs or foam imitations. Their feet are halved corks, their lances wooden skewers and their hair is made from lengths of thick rug wool, stuck on at right angles for an 'Afro' hair-style.

Jumping jacks

These little figures make really special gifts for children because they are fun to play with. If you pull the jumping jack's string it will jump about and wave its arms and legs in an amusing way.

The actual mechanism is quite simple, but the figures need to be made carefully and there are two points to consider while they are being put together. First, the technique of making the arms and legs move depends on accuracy of cutting and fitting and, secondly, they need to be carefully decorated so that each one has a convincing and recognizable character.

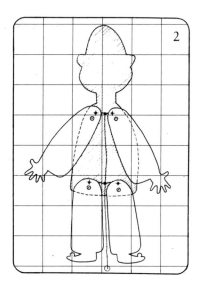

Key to symbols	1

✦   hole for string

⊙   hole for paperclip

⊘   wood screw

Ⓡ   drawing pin (thumbtack)

⊓   string clip

φ   ring hook

⌂   hanger

Ａ   striking block

Ｗ   spacing block

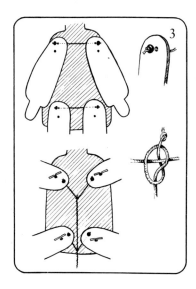

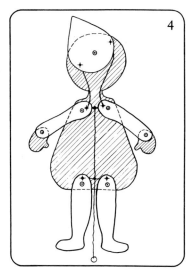

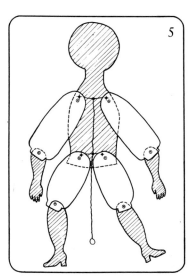

Instructions for making the jumping jacks are given on these pages. Pull the string, and the legs and arms wave about wildly.

To make a jumping jack, first copy diagram no. 2 (opposite) on squared paper. In this way you can make the figure whatever size you like—the larger the squares, the larger the figure will finally be. Make sure to keep the proportions of the figures as shown. The next stage is to transfer to the drawing all the symbols for holes, staples, drawing pins, and all the other little bits and pieces needed to make the model move. The diagram on the page opposite gives the key for the figure diagrams.

Cutting out

Use carbon paper to transfer the drawing to thin card (pasteboard), and then cut out the parts. Put the parts together, using paper clips for the joints, and see how it all fits. This is just a routine check to make sure the parts are all the right size and that the figure will work when it is assembled.

If it works satisfactorily, you can now use these card (pasteboard) templates as patterns with which to cut the figures out of plywood, 3mm ($\frac{1}{8}$in.) thick, with a fretsaw. Smooth down all the edges with sandpaper and drill all the holes as marked, with a 1.5mm ($\frac{1}{16}$in.) twist drill.

Painting the figures

To paint the figures, use poster paints. First apply a base coat of white. Leave this to dry and rub down with fine sandpaper before the final painting. Put in all the features and intricate parts of the decoration with an artist's sable brush and indian ink so that the lines are very fine. A good, even coat of varnish on the front and edges of the figure will protect the poster paint.

You may prefer to use oil-based enamel paints, which can often be bought from crafts shops in very small tins in a wide range of bright colors. Here again, give an undercoat of white, leave it to dry and rub it down with fine sandpaper before final painting. With enamel paints it should not be necessary to add a coat of varnish, but the fine detail will have to be painted in the same enamel paint, not with indian ink, as ink will not stick to a shiny surface.

Acrylic paints can also be used, and these have the advantage of drying quickly yet forming a hard surface. These paints can be varnished.

When the jumping jacks are really dry, lay the pieces painted side down on a soft, clean surface. (A table top covered in layers of newspaper, over which a sheet of plastic has been spread, would be ideal.) Clean off the backs of the figures to remove paint or varnish splashes. Open up any varnish or paint-filled holes. Polish the figures with colorless wax to make sure of easy movement.

An alternative way of decorating jumping jacks is to paint the arms, legs and faces but add fabric clothes and woollen hair, funny fur hats and so on.

The diagram (bottom right, page 102) shows how the legs and arms are joined together in the resting position with fine, strong string and how to tie the pulling string to the connecting strings. The center diagram at the bottom of page 102 gives detailed stringing instructions for each figure. Slip small wooden beads on the end of the string to hold the figure away from the wall on which it will be hanging.

Fasten the limbs loosely to the body with round-headed paper fasteners.

Lastly, knot the pulling string to the strings joining each arm and leg, and, when you have attached the jacks to the wall, they will be ready to start jumping.

Press down the lever on the tender and the fireman disappears, the driver turns round, and smoke belches from the chimney.

The steam train

This delightful toy holds a few surprises. You cannot see at first which parts move, but when the lever at the back is pressed, the fireman disappears from the tender, the engine-driver, who has a double head, looks out of the back of his cab, and a big puff of black smoke comes out of the chimney. At the same time, a typical steam engine noise is produced by the friction of the wooden parts against each other.

To make this steam train, copy the diagram opposite on squared paper, as for the jumping jacks, making it whatever size you like. The model is three-layered, so you will need two identical engine shapes and one moving part, as in the diagram. Cut them out in thin card (pasteboard) first, to make sure the parts will all work, and then, using the card (pasteboard) templates as patterns, cut the shapes out of 3mm (⅛in.) plywood with a fretsaw. Smooth all the edges with sandpaper and drill a hole where marked. Paint the engine sides. A paper fastener joins the three sections at the pivoting point. The far side of the train is screwed from the back into spacers (W) which are glued inside. Hang the train from two staples.

Working with felt

Felt is a marvellous material for toymaking. It is easy to sew and it does not need to be hemmed. It comes in a wide range of colors, is reversible and can be glued as well as sewn. Here are some colorful ideas for gifts in felt.

Christmas stocking

To make this attractive stocking, you need two 250mm (10in.) squares of blue felt, felt scraps in pink, light blue, white and green, and a plastic curtain ring.

Make a paper pattern for the stocking shape. Pin this to the blue felt squares and cut it out. Sew a 40mm (1½in.) wide strip of pink felt to the upper edge of the stocking and sew hearts, circles and leaves to the main body. Sew the two sides of the stocking together, right side out, including a felt loop at the top with the curtain ring attached. Trim around the stocking with pinking shears.

Santa Claus

You will need two 250mm (10in.) squares of red felt, black, white and pink scraps, cotton wool (absorbent cotton) and a plastic curtain ring.

This figure is basically a triangle of red felt with a 150mm (6in.) base and 200mm (8in.) sides. Mark out the pattern on brown paper, then pin it to the felt. Cut out a triangle, a cap,

arms, pockets and belt from red felt. Lay the two squares of red felt on top of each other, so that you can cut out the fronts and backs at the same time. This will ensure that they are exactly the same size.

Stitch stripes made out of white felt scraps on to the cap, cuffs and hem of Santa Claus's jacket. Then add belt and buttons in black. Cut out his black boots. Sew up the arms, cap and boots and stuff them lightly with cotton wool (absorbent cotton).

When making the cap, do not forget to include the loop with the curtain ring in it so that the figure can be hung up.

Cut out simple hand shapes and a circular face from two layers of pink felt and glue on the mouth, eyes and cheeks. Glue the face to the top of the triangle forming the coat and sew the hands on to the arms. Then push the cap over the top of the face, and stitch it in place.

Add a white cotton beard.

Finally, sew together the two triangles forming the body, including the arms and boots in the seams at the right places.

Make a 50mm (2in.) slit in the back triangle as high up as possible and fill the Santa Claus with small sweets.

Tea or coffee cozy

The cozy above is for a pot measuring 300mm (12in.) wide and 340mm (13½in.) high. You

Sewing with felt needs no hemming along the edges. All the items in this photograph are easy to make and lively and bright.

need two pieces of foam 350mm (14in.) square, green, dark and light blue felt and lining material. The blue strip around the cozy is 50mm (2in.) wide and about 860mm (34in.) long.

Cut a paper pattern for the two main panels, rounding off the top symmetrically. Cut out. Trim the two pieces of foam to measure 10mm (⅜in.) less all around than the felt. With tailor's chalk, divide each green panel into squares as shown. Pin the felt to the foam and sew along the chalk lines to join them. Sew the blue side-panel in between, turn the lower edges inside and hand-stitch. Pinch the felt loop between the two green panels and sew from the inside. Make a soft lining to the same pattern, push it into the cozy and slip-stitch in place. Stick on felt leaves and flowers.

Egg cozies are made the same way, but reduce the pattern to about a quarter of the size.

For an oven glove, draw around your hand on paper as for a mitten. Allow about 25mm (1in.) extra all around. Sew together, stick on flowers and trim with pinking shears.

Ladybird

You will need red and black felt scraps, two small black beads and stuffing.

For the head, cut a circle of black felt about 45mm (1¾in.) in diameter. Cut it in half and

sew the two halves together leaving the straight side open. Turn inside out and stuff. Close the gap and sew on bead eyes. Cut two circles of black felt about 120mm (4¾in.) in diameter and sew together, taking in the head and leaving a gap for stuffing. Cut two circles of red felt, about 125mm (5in.) diameter, cut them in half and sew together for double thickness wings. Sew these on the larger black circle and glue on spots. Stuff the body with sand or rice and sew up the gap.

Frog

You need dark and light green felt scraps, two green glass beads and stuffing. Cut two frog bodies, using the pattern below. Stitch them together, leaving a small opening for turning and stuffing with sand or rice. Don't stuff too tightly. Close the opening and sew on bead eyes. The other items in the picture can all be made from felt scraps, using the techniques described.

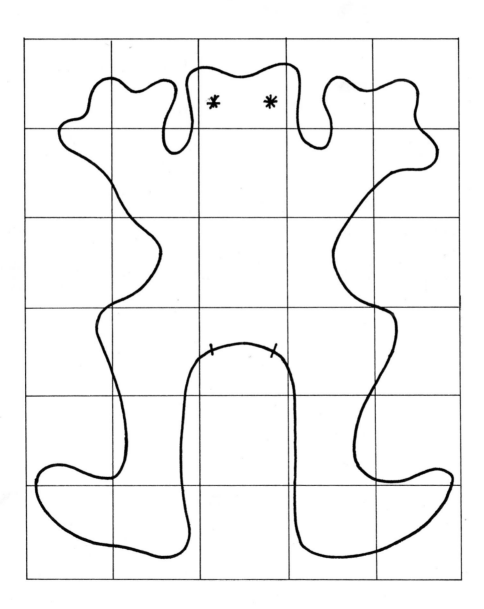

Pattern (same size) for the frog shown in the photograph on page 108.

Knitted glove puppets

For the clothing you need 40g (1½oz.) of yarn and for the head and hands, 12g (½oz.) of yarn. The hair is made of oddments of yarn. Knit the clothes according to the diagram (right) and make a 20mm (¾in.) hem on the lower edges. To make the hands, pick up the stitches on the ends of the sleeves on four needles and knit for 35mm (1⅜in.) in stocking stitch, then on the next row knit two together all around. Draw up the remaining stitches.

For the heads, pick up the stitches around the neck of the clothing on four needles. Work five rounds in k.1 p.1 rib. Sixth round: knit together every other stitch. Seventh and eighth rounds:

knit. Ninth round: Knit together every third stitch. Continue for 80mm (3⅛in.), then insert a 70mm (2¾in.) polystyrene ball and draw up the stitches.

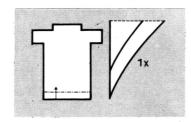

Pattern for the body and head- and neck-scarves for the two glove puppets.

110

To give a finger grip, bore into the base of the ball with the end of a wooden spoon.

To make the hair, sew on bundles of yarn, cutting the girl's hair into a fringe at the front and plaiting the remainder. Glue on fabric eyes and rosy cheeks. Embroider mouths and noses. Hem the edges of the scarves.

Pompon figures

To make pompons, cut two disks the same size, from a piece of card (pasteboard), each with a fairly large hole in the middle. Lay the disks one on top of the other and cut a slit through to make it easier to wind on the wool. Wind from one side of the slit to the other and then back again. (See the photographs on page 113.)

Wind around with yarn until the center hole is filled up. When the winding is complete, cut through the threads all around the edge of the disks and separate the two pieces slightly. Take a length of double wool and bind the pompon very tightly around its middle between the card (pasteboard) disks. Remove the disks and trim off surplus wool.

When several pompons are to be joined together to make a whole, as for example in the body of the dog above, join the pompons together and then trim them to the required shape

All the animals in this zoo are based on pompons. You can make them in many different colors and sizes.

until the divisions between them can no longer be seen, but make the pompons bigger than usual to allow for loss of wool in trimming.

The long figures (page 111) are made by binding the pompons firmly with string, then laying them together so that a strong thread can be run through them all and knotted securely at either end.

Pompon zoo

Diagrams for beaks, ears, feet and so on are on page 114. Make them out of felt. All these finishing touches should be glued firmly to the in-side of the pompon (part the wool to get the glue spread on). Pipe cleaner legs especially need plenty of glue. Stand the figures upside down while the glue dries.

To make oval pompons, first make a round one with a diameter equal to the length of the required shape, then trim it to an oval. To make a figure stand firmly (like the duck and the lady-bird above), trim the pompons flat on the un-derside of the figure.

Parrot

Trim the body to make an oval and join to the head pompon. Cut out the additional trimmings following the diagram on the opposite page. *A* is the wings, *B* the tail, *C* the beak, *D* the eyes.

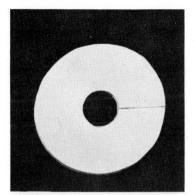

Make the mouse, snake, dog and little boy from pompons. Use felt for the eyes and ears, and a bead or button for the nose.

Monkey

Trim the body to an oval. The head is a ball pompon and the muzzle is a smaller ball pompon, cut flat on one side. The mouth is a piece of yarn sewn on to the muzzle. For arms and legs, take 18 thicknesses of yarn and thread them through the body, then plait them and knot the ends. Trim to form a tassel.

Birds

Two joined pompons with pipe cleaner legs.

Fish

Wind different colors on to the disk in layers for a striped effect. Fins and tail are wool loops.

Ladybird

Trim the body flat where the head is to be attached. Bind the body with black wool to mark the wings. Make plaited wool feelers.

On page 114: (shown in black) *Diagrams for the beaks, ears and feet of the zoo animals;* (shown in red): *Diagrams for the parrot A = wings; B = tail; C = beak; D = eyes. Cut two of each piece.*

Cut two of each. Lay the wing pieces together, small on top, matching dots. Oversew the edges, padding with a little cotton wool (absorbent cotton). Sew the two tail pieces together around the straight edges, leaving the bottom-shaped part open. Insert some strands of wool and glue in place. Sew the beak pieces together and stuff firmly. Make pipe cleaner legs and glue in place.

BIRDS   MONKEY   CHICK   MOUSE   DUCK

Tail 1x

Beak 2x

Ear 2x

Beak 2x

Eye 2x

Ear 2x

Beak 2x

Eye 2x

2x   Eyes   2x

FISH

Mouth 2x

Foot 4x

Eye 2x

Eyes 2x

Eye 2x

FROG   RABBIT

Mouth 2x

Eye 2x

Wing 2x   Eye 2x

Foot 2x

Ear 2x

Beak 2x

Foot 4x

PENGUIN

Eyes

2x   2x   Spot 4x

LADYBIRD

B   A   A   A

D   C

D

When decorating these bags, try to show their fragrance in some way. A flower-patterned ribbon is sewn to one of the bags shown here. Make the lace rose by gathering up a length of lace trimming. Wind it very tight, secure it with a few stitches, and sew a pearl droplet in the center.

It is very easy to make delightful scents and fragrances, and give cupboards, closets, drawers and rooms in your home fresh, subtle aromas. Some mixtures come from ancient recipes. Here are a few you can try yourself. (You will have to obtain some ingredients from herbalists' shops or pharmacies.)

Sweet-scented bags

These little sweet-scented bags are very simple to make. You need pieces of closely woven fabric, various trimmings, beads, dried flowers or embroidery silks, small rubber bands and the in-gredients listed. To make a bag, cut two pieces of fabric 100 × 125mm (4 × 5in.). With right sides facing one another, sew three seams, leaving one of the narrow ends open. Neaten the open edge, turn the bag inside out, press and attach the trimmings. The finished bag measures about 75 × 100mm (3 × 4in.).

Lavender bags

4 tblsp dried lavender flowers
½ teasp orris root powder
3 drops lavender oil

Rose bags

4 tblsp dried rose petals
½ teasp orris root powder
8 drops rose oil
   Put the ingredients in a bowl, mix thoroughly and divide between two bags. Close each bag

Sweet-smelling citrus pomanders make an ideal gift. In the past they were originally made from ambergris, musk, civet, etc. The mixture was enclosed in an ornate crystal, gold or silver case and hung from a bracelet, necklace or belt.

with a rubber band, then cover the band with pretty cord or a ribbon and bow.

Citrus pomanders

These citrus pomanders are stuck with whole cloves and carefully rolled in a mixture of fixatives and finely ground herbs or spices. To make these pomanders, you will need:

2 thin skinned citrus fruits (oranges, lemons or limes)
85g (3oz.) whole cloves
1 tblsp orris root powder
1 tblsp ground cinnamon
wooden cocktail sticks
trimming to decorate

If you wish to tie a ribbon round the pomander, leave a wide channel when pressing the cloves directly into the fruit. If the skin is rather thick, the clove tops may break. If this happens, make holes with a cocktail stick first.

Mix the orris root powder and ground cinnamon in a small bowl, pressing out any lumps with the back of a spoon. Roll the clove-covered fruit in the spice mixture, then wrap it in tissue paper and leave it among the clothes in a closed cupboard (closet) or drawer for four weeks.

The pomander is now partially dried out. Blow off any excess powder and then decorate it with ribbons, lace, dried flowers or any pretty item.

Pot-pourri

A pot-pourri can contain any pleasant-smelling flower, herb or spice. Roses make up most of the

All the ingredients for this pot-pourri must be quite dry before use. Pick roses and other flowers just before they are fully-bloomed, on a dry day, after the dew has evaporated and before the sun becomes too hot. Use only blemish-free petals. Pull them gently from the flower-head and dry them in a warm, airy room on a piece of absorbent fabric stretched between two chair-backs. Pick herbs just before they bloom and dry them in the same way.

mixture and other dried flowers, nasturtiums, borage, cornflowers and marigold petals can be included to add splashes of bright color.

To make this pot-pourri, you will need:
4 cups dried rose petals
2 cups dried rose geranium leaves
1 cup dried lavender flowers
1 cup dried elderflowers
2 tblsp ground dried orange peel
2 teasp freshly ground cloves
2 teasp freshly ground allspice

2 teasp freshly ground cardamom seeds
1 tblsp everlasting flowers
2 tblsp orris root powder
1 teasp rose oil
½ teasp sandalwood oil
3 drops lavender oil

Mix the ingredients in a large basin, adding the orris root powder and oils last. Cover the basin and leave to mature in a dry, dark place for three weeks. Stir the mixture occasionally.

Transfer the pot-pourri to pretty lidded bowls or dishes. Remove the lids when you want to fill your rooms with subtle fragrances.

Fragrant powder sachets

These little sachets are filled with fragrant ingredients which are all ground to a rough powder. The sachets will lie flat and can be tacked to the lining of coats, jackets or hats. They can

You can buy the ingredients for these fragrant powder sachets from herbalists, but you can also pick and dry some of them. Potted rose geraniums are to be found in most gardening centers, and you can easily take cuttings. Lavender is a common garden plant; gather the flowers on a dry day, and dry and store them in airtight jars.

also be placed inside a writing box to give the envelopes a delicate perfume.

Any finely woven fabric is used to make the sachet, which is usually about 100mm (4in.) square. It is embroidered, decorated with ribbons or lace, or if it is to be hidden inside a garment, left plain.

To make a sweet fragrance, you will need:
1 tblsp ground lavender flowers
1 tblsp ground elderflowers
1 tblsp ground rose geranium leaves
1 tblsp orris root powder
1 tblsp powdered gum benzoin
1 tblsp sandalwood powder
2 teasp fine salt
4 drops bergamot oil
4 drops ambergris oil

Grind all the ingredients to a rough powder and mix them in a bowl, pressing out any small lumps with the back of a spoon. Put 2–3 tablespoons of powder into each sachet.

The lamp, hand mirror, large mirror and casket are examples of plain objects enhanced by skilful découpage.

Découpage

Small items of furniture decorated with cut-out paper prints protected by layers of varnish make charming and unusual gifts.

All kinds of things can be decorated with découpage (a French word meaning cutting out)—trays, boxes, frames, table mats—almost anything so long as it has a firm and durable surface. It is an excellent way of refurbishing old objects, such as the mirror frame above.

With the many prints available, there is no lack of suitable material with which to decorate such objects, and the other items needed are cheap and easily obtainable.

Finding the right prints

Choose prints with a clear outline, since these make for easier cutting out. Make a collection of printed wrapping papers (ideal for large-scale undertakings), magazine illustrations, catalogue prints, posters, reproductions of museum prints and even greetings cards, though if you do use cards of any kind the backing must be soaked

Four boxes, each with a design suited to its own character. When making a box as a gift, take the recipient's taste into account.

off before using them so that the print is not too thick.

Keep prints flat in folders, filing them in various categories to save time searching.

Colors

The boxes and trays etc. to which the prints are to be glued can look more attractive when given a coat of base color, though they can also be left in their natural state if the wood is good enough. Paint them with emulsion, acrylic or oil-based gloss paints. Wooden surfaces, like that of the green salt box above, can be stained instead of painted. Though most prints are bought ready-colored, some people prefer to color their own and for this crayons are recommended, since the colors do not run easily and their sharp points can get into the corners of a tricky design. Watercolors can also be used, and inks or fiber-tip pens, but these colors must be well sealed before being varnished, or they will run.

Other items and materials needed

Brushes. Buy good ones, as poor-quality brushes shed their hairs. Use separate ones for painting the object and for varnishing. Clean brushes well after use and dry them.

Scissors. The finer and more delicate the print is cut, the more effective the finished work will be, so scissors must be sharp.

Adhesive. This is for gluing down prints. Use one made especially for gluing paper.

Sealer. An essential, for if the print is not sealed after being glued down, varnish will seep into it and ruin the découpage. Acrylic sealer can be bought in spray cans or you can use slightly thinned white PVA glue (which dries clear). Note though that this type of sealer can change the base color of an object, so either go over the whole design and the object with it, or just cover the design, taking care not to overlap the base color.

Varnish. Special, very clear découpage varnishes can be bought from crafts shops, but they are expensive, and ordinary polyurethane varnish works very well as long as you do not mind the slightly yellow effect it gives. Varnish forms a skin quickly after the tin is opened, so buy small

Table mats offer suitable surfaces for découpage. Seal the edges carefully; they will be wiped clean with a damp cloth and must be watertight.

tins, close the lids firmly after use and then turn the tin upside down.

You will also need a ruler and pencil for positioning prints, a lint-free cloth for dusting, white spirit (alcohol) for cleaning brushes, fine sandpaper or 'wet and dry' paper for sanding down between coats of varnish, steel wool for the final finish and wax polish.

How to work

Prepare the object to be decorated. If it is wooden, sandpaper it well, filling in cracks with a filler. A very bad surface can be given a coat of gesso or be covered with paper. Lids should be removed from boxes and doors from cupboards, and these should be treated separately.

Paint the object, making sure that the surface is well covered, otherwise flaws will show up later.

Cutting out

If the prints are uncolored, color and then seal them before cutting out. In any case, sealing a print before cutting it out helps to strengthen the paper and so prevents it from tearing. Cut crisply, well into the corners. Turn the paper and feed it to the scissors rather than trying to force the scissors around the corners. Cut large awkward pieces at a point where the cuts will not show, then cut out the detail, and glue down the whole design.

Planning the design

Cut plenty of pieces, as this helps in the planning of the design. Lay the pieces on the object, mov-

Old prints come to life when well varnished.

ing them about until you have a pleasing design. On the side of a box, you can get a rough idea of how the design will look when finished by sticking the pieces on temporarily with weak glue. Lightly mark in pencil where the pieces are to go.

Coat the surface of the object with glue and press down the paper cut-out on the surface, pushing with the fingers toward the edges of each piece until all the surplus glue is squeezed out and there are no air bubbles. Check that all outside edges are firmly glued and all the air bubbles are gone. If you do find an air bubble after the glue has dried, cut into it and glue it again.

When gluing large areas of paper (as for example on the table mats on page 121) dampen the paper with water before gluing and this will help prevent air bubbles and wrinkles forming.

Varnishing

Varnish in a dry, dust-free room, and work in a good light. Seal the design and allow it to dry.

Below: *An ordinary bin makes an excellent rubbish (trash) can when worked carefully, as here.*

Wipe off dust and lint. Apply about eight coats of varnish, putting it on with flowing strokes. At the end of each coat go around the corners and edges carefully with a brush, to make sure there are no runs. If any runs do set hard, sand them smooth before applying the next coat. Watch out for brush-hairs and remove those too. Dark backgrounds show flaws less clearly than light ones. Allow each coat of varnish to dry thoroughly before applying the next.

When the design has been well protected by eight or so coats of varnish, it has to be sand-papered between succeeding coats, in order to sink the design below the level of the varnish and to get an even finish. Rub down with fine sand-paper or 'wet and dry' paper wrapped around a sanding block. Wipe down the surface after each sandpapering with a soapy cloth and water, dry and then revarnish.

Finishing

Rub down with steel wool, then rub wax polish into the surface until there is a good bloom. A quick way of finishing is to rub down with 'wet and dry' paper, then apply a coat of semi-matt varnish, to take off the high gloss sheen. To get an 'antique' effect, as in the two pictures above, you need a special liquid, obtainable from crafts shops, which is applied to the surface of the print with a brush. Brown paint is then rubbed into the print and the edges.

Compatible materials

COLORS PAINTS GLUES VARNISH	Water colors	Poster paints	Gouache	Acrylic paints	Synthetic enamel (model paints)	Printer's colors (oil-based)	Printer's colors (water-soluble)	Fiber-tip pens	Clear fast-drying glue (synthetic resin)	Synthetic rubber resin (impact)	PVA glue	Acid-free glue	Poly-urethane varnish
MATERIALS													
Dried flowers	yes	yes	yes	yes	no	no	no	no	yes	no	no	yes	no
Fabrics	no	no	no	no	no	yes	yes	no	yes	no	yes	no	no
Leaves	no	no	no	no	no	no	no	no	no	no	no	yes	no
Metals	no	no	no	yes	yes	yes	no	yes	yes	yes	no	no	yes
Paper and cardboard	yes	yes	yes	yes	no	yes	yes	yes	yes	yes	yes	no	yes
Wood and seeds	yes	yes	yes	yes	yes	yes	yes	yes	yes	yes	yes	yes	yes
Undercoat/ primer	yes	yes	yes	—	with wood: yes	—	—	—	—	—	—	—	—
Thinner	water	water	water	water	special purpose thinner	white spirit (alcohol)	water	—	—	—	water	—	white spirit (alcohol)
Lacquer	colorless varnish	colorless varnish or wax	colorless varnish	varnish	—	—	—	varnish	—	—	—	—	—

PLEASE NOTE: This tabular summary is intended only as a rough guide to possibilities. Always follow the instructions and warnings accompanying materials, colors and glues, and whenever possible consult your crafts supplier, art materials dealer and other experts. This is especially important in the case of solvents or thinners and lacquers or varnishes. The composition of materials and paints varies from country to country, and maker to maker. Always try out colors and materials, and all mixtures and solutions before beginning work.

Acknowledgements

Acknowledgements and thanks are due to the following authors, photographers and artists for illustrations previously used in the following publications:

Advents und Weihnachtsgestecke by Heim Apel and Margret Glende. Photos Toni Schneiders. Drawings Herbert Becker. (*Christophorus-Verlag*). Pages 8–14, 15 (*below*), 17–18 (*left*), 20 (*left*), 22. *Figuren aus Tannenzapfen* by Ruth Dürr. Photos Toni Schneiders. (*Christophorus-Verlag*). Pages 14 (*right*), 15 (*above*), 20 (*left*), 77–8. *Aparter Zimmerschmuck* by Hein Apel and Margret Glende. Photos Toni Schneiders. Drawings Herbert Becker. (*Christophorus-Verlag*). Pages 16, 18 (*right*), 19–20 (*right*), 21. *Candle Making* by Anne Collings, David Constable and Randall Marr. Photos Robert Harding (page 26, *bottom right*, Des Parker; page 28, *top left*, Mina Rasheed). Drawings Colin Elgie. (*Search Press*). Pages 23–9. *Tinfoil Decorations (Weihnachtliches aus Goldpapier)*. Text and drawings Brigitte Schüssler. Photos Fernard Rausser (page 30 and title page), Tony Schneiders (page 31, *left*), K W Schüssler (page 31, *right*). (*Search Press* and *Christophorus-Verlag*). Pages 30–1, 39–43, 49–53, 73–4. *Minispan und Finnspan* by Elisabeth Hammer. Photos Toni Schneiders. (*Christophorus-Verlag*). Pages 32–4. *Neue Strohsterne und Engel* by Gretl Zimmermann. Photos Maximilian Rusch. Drawings Maria Holzinger and Alfred Kutschera. (*Christophorus-Verlag*). Pages 35–8, 54–7. *Bunte Kugeln*. Text, drawings and photos Werner Roll. (*Christophorus-Verlag*). Pages 44–8. *Adventkalender und Weihnachtsschmuck*.

Text and drawings Agnes Gaensslen. Photos Toni Schneiders. (*Christophorus-Verlag*). Pages 58–63. *Cloth Sculpture*. Text, models and drawings Sheila Franklin. Photos Jeet Jain. (*Search Press*). Pages 64–8. *Christmas Cribs (Unsere Hauskrippe)*. Text Hein and Maria Apel, adapted by Christian Albrecht. Photos Toni Schneiders. Drawings Hein Apel. (*Search Press* and *Christophorus-Verlag*). Pages 69–72. *Kleine Krippenwerkstatt* by Bruno Epple. Photos Toni Schneiders. (*Christophorus-Verlag*). Pages 75–7. *Strohsterne* by Marta Högeman and Erich Priester. Models Schwester Responsa. Photos Toni Schneiders. Drawings Roland Ruff. (*Christophorus-Verlag*). Pages 79–80. *Christmas Cards*. Text and models Martin Bristow. Photos Search Press Studios. (*Search Press*). Pages 81–9. *Paper Chains*. Text and diagrams Bill Leeson. Photos Search Press Studios. (*Search Press*). Pages 90–9. *Fun Figures (Pop-Figuren als Tischschmuck)*. Text and photos Werner Roll. (*Search Press* and *Christophorus-Verlag*). Pages 100–1. *Lustige Hampelfiguren*. Text and drawings Paul-Heinrich Dingler. Photos Toni Schneiders. (*Christophorus-Verlag*). Pages 102–5. *Filz Kunterbund*. Text and drawings Elke Schäfer. Photos Toni Schneiders. (*Christophorus-Verlag*). Pages 106–9. *Woolly Toys (Tiere und Puppen aus Wolle)*. Text and drawings Erna Rath. Photos Toni Schneiders. (*Christophorus-Verlag*). Pages 110–14. *Scents and Fragrances* by Polly Pinder. Photos Jeet Jain. (*Search Press*). Pages 115–18. *Découpage* by Valerie Jackson and Joan Pilton. Photos Hawkley Studio Associates. (*Search Press*). Pages 119–23.

Index

OTHER CRAFT TITLES

MAGNIFICENT PATCHWORK
by Marie-Janine Solvit

For every needlecraft enthusiast. 50 original designs for bedspreads, cushions, wall-hangings, and many other useful items for the home.

THE SPLENDID SOFT TOY BOOK

The Splendid Soft Toy Book contains a wealth of ideas and pictures for making a wide variety of toys and dolls, from a green corduroy crocodile to detailed traditional, even collectors' dolls. More than 60 full colour pictures and over 70 black and white illustrations show the reader how to fashion appealing figures and animals of all shapes and sizes.
Cased and paperback.

HOW TO MAKE BEAUTIFUL FLOWERS
edited by Valerie Jackson

How to make flowers from all sorts of materials; silk, paper, shells, bread dough, feathers, seeds. The instructions are simple, the materials inexpensive and easy to obtain.

HOMEMADE and at a fraction of the cost
by Polly Pinder

'An imaginative and practical book full of ideas, recipes and instructions for making breads, chutneys, drinks, sweets, soft cheese, soaps. Superb colour photographs.' *The Lady*.
Cased and paperback.

THE CHRISTMAS CRAFTS BOOK

Creative ideas and designs for the whole family to make objects with a Christmas flavour: table and room decorations, stars, Christmas tree ornaments, candles and candlesticks, angels, nativity scenes, paper chains and Christmas cards.

COLOURCRAFT

Hundreds of simple ideas, designs and ways of using colour to express your natural creativity and imagination.

NATURECRAFT

A crafts book for all who love the colour, shape and texture of natural materials.

MADE TO TREASURE
Embroideries for all Occasions edited by Kit Pyman.

This book offers a rich variety of ideas for embroideries to be made to commemorate special occasions – christenings, weddings, birthdays – from simple greetings cards to a gold-work panel for a golden wedding. A heart warming present precisely because it is specially made.

EVERY KIND OF PATCHWORK
edited by Kit Pyman

'Really lives up to its title, and is sufficiently easy to follow that even the most helpless needleperson would be tempted to have a go. But there's plenty, too, for the experienced.' *The Guardian*.
Cased and Paperback.

DECORATING CAKES FOR CHILDREN'S PARTIES
by Polly Pinder

Thirty-one cakes tastefully illustrated in full colour plus 424 step-by-step drawings that will inspire the reader to make these stunning and delightful cakes. Cake ideas include Humpty Dumpty, Superman, Winnie-the-Pooh, Fast-food addict.

If you are interested in any of the above books or any of the art and craft titles published by Search Press please send for free catalogue to: Search Press Ltd., Dept B, Wellwood, North Farm Road, Tunbridge Wells, Kent. TN2 3DR.